MARY— GOD'S MOTHER and OURS

by Pope Paul VI

ST. PAUL EDITIONS

Grateful acknowledgment is made to the
following for use of translations in this book:

L'Osservatore Romano (OR)
    English Edition
    Vatican City

The Pope Speaks (TPS)
    Church Documents Quarterly
    Washington, D.C.

Library of Congress Cataloging in Publication Data

Paulus VI, Pope, 1897-1978
    Mary—God's Mother and Ours.

    1. Mary, Virgin—Addresses, essays, lectures.
I. Daughters of St. Paul.   II. Title.
BT602.P37   232.91   79-14736

Printed in the U.S.A. by the Daughters of St. Paul
50 St. Paul's Ave., Boston, Ma. 02130

The Daughters of St. Paul are an international congregation
of religious women serving the Church with the communi-
cations media.

CONTENTS

Marian Devotion for the Modern Christian

Dear sons and daughters! We are happy to be among you this morning, to offer the holy Mass for you and with you, and to join in the solemn homage which the Marian congregations wish to render to the holy Virgin upon the occasion of the fourth centenary of the foundation of the *"Prima Primaria"* congregation, right here where that pious association was born, where it has trained in piety and Christian life so many generations of Roman youth, and whence have radiated throughout the entire world the light of its constitutions, its examples, its experiences; and everything has just been crowned with testimony of the loftiest virtues and the most sincere fidelity to Christ and to His Church.

MEMBERSHIP DURING YOUTH

This meeting arouses in our mind a pleasant memory from the distant years of our adolescence and youth, namely that of our membership in the Marian Congregation of the Jesuit Fathers who were at that time in charge of the Arici College at Brescia. They still deserve our affectionate and constant gratitude.

In addition, we have the happy opportunity of greeting all of this magnificent assembly surrounding us, which has met under the august and familiar name of Virgin Mary. What a joy it is for us to see so many men and women celebrating the glory of the Mother of God; what sweet emotion it is for us to listen to your resounding voices blending in a single prayer, a single song destined for the Queen of Heaven! We are not unaware of the problems of the life of present-day generations. How great a subject for admiration and reflection it is for us, then, to know that your generation is polarized around the Blessed Virgin who gave us Christ and takes as a basis for its spirituality devotion to the mysteries and virtues of Jesus and Mary. We wish you to know the inner satisfaction of being witness to this and we want to greet in you all of the Marian congregations to which you belong and which you represent.

MARIAN PIETY IN MODERN CHRISTIAN LIFE

First of all, we want to fix our attention and yours on the pedagogical efficacy of Marian piety in the sensitive and difficult work of educating modern man to Christian life.

And on that subject, it seems to us that one must emphasize above all the religious wealth that devotion to Mary, so genuine and sincere, as yours is, adds to the soul of men who are struggling with the great experiences, or indeed the problems and crises that life brings to them. Is it not true that devotion to the Virgin commits the entire human being to the act of faith upon which the whole spiritual edifice of Christian life rests, namely, exact and concrete knowledge of the basic religious truths of the Gospel and the catechism, a will nourished by the filial love that such a Mother easily awakens in hearts, and the whole train of the simplest, sweetest, purest and most beautiful feelings that the mystery of the Incarnation authorizes us to transport from the human to the religious sphere?

And the doctrine—that is, the basic religious reality—of Marian piety, is it not the most orthodox and the most fruitful of Catholic spirituality when it places us in contact with the divine thought regarding Mary, chosen to be the Mother of our Savior Jesus Christ?

A SOURCE OF MORAL VALUES

This religious wealth of Marian devotion provides an inexhaustible and magnificent source of moral values which can give strength to the men of today and an experience capable of contributing incomparable fullness to their lives.

What are human beings, and especially the young, seeking in life?

A SEARCH FOR BEAUTY...

They are seeking beauty: now, Mary is the epitome of beauty. Masterpieces are never partial beauties, but a synthesis of the beautiful: Mary is the creature most clearly revealing the divine trinitarian presence: "Him whom the heavens were unable to hold you enclosed in your bosom." A human presence also: Mary is the new Eve in whom the destiny of all living persons is found.

Beauty is a transparent expression: all of the arts have sought to express it and have expressed it in the masterpieces of all centuries. Beauty is a restful gift: Mary, amid the torments of life, calms all worries of the flesh, of the mind, and of social life.

...FOR GRANDEUR

They are seeking grandeur: their law is to grow, they are feverish to surpass all bounds. Mary has passed all ordinary bounds, but in the direction of grandeur; and for this reason she has become the only human creature who was able to say: "...all generations shall call me blessed." [1]

...FOR JOY

They are seeking joy: "Your birth, O Mary, was an occasion of joy for the whole world," the passing from an "economy" of curses to one of blessings, from a world of constant errors, to one in which one breathes fully the freedom of adopted sons.

...AND LOVE

They are seeking love: that is, a total communion between two persons, according to God's plan of creation by which woman is intended to give life and to be the companion of man, the head of the home. Mary, who at Cana wished that nothing of the exaltation of love be lost, shows men where they may contemplate the highest feminine ideal — in virginity and in maternity, both impregnated with her beauty and the fullness of grace.

...A SEARCH FOR MARY

Thus Mary is for everyone the source of true beauty, of true grandeur, of true joy, and of true love. But where will you find Mary? Surely not in exaggerations, nor in sentimentalism, nor in the misuse of deductions for the purpose of emphasis and hyperbole, nor in novelty. As Pope John XXIII, our predecessor of pleasant memory, expressed it:

"Consequently, all Catholics are children of our Lady and their piety for Mary should reflect this common membership in the family of the children of God, expressed always by the habitual signs of the centuries-old worship devoted by the Church of Jesus Christ to the Mother of the Savior. So, dear children, avoid everything that sets one apart; seek, rather, that Marian devotion which is the most confirmed by tradition, as it has been transmitted to us since the beginning through the prayers of successive generations of Christians in the

Orient and Occident. Such piety towards the most holy Virgin is the mark of a truly Catholic heart."[2]

Dear sons and daughters, it is in the history of salvation, in the Gospel, that you will find Mary, as well as in the treasures of the liturgy which transmits the great heritage of the Church's thought and prayer. You will also find her in the humble family traditions of Christian families, in particular in the rosary. You will also find her in your daily effort always to see in every woman the holy Virgin Mary, and hence, far removed from the inhuman and excessive obsession of the senses, the most elevated collaboration with God's plan.

TRANSFORMING MAN'S DAILY WORLD

The most beautiful task of the Marian congregations will be to establish this essential, transforming relationship with the daily world of modern man. When all is said and done, you will find Mary if you take scrupulous care to place her within the whole of the Christian mystery, for devotion to Mary is not an end in itself, but the main road leading you to Christ, and in Him to the glory of God and the love of the Church.

That, dear sons and daughters, is the wish that we want to express with all our heart, for you and all of the Marian congregations that you represent.

Be faithful devotees of Mary, who will make of you good sons of the Church and true apostles of Christ.

This is the intention for which we gladly call upon you abundant divine grace, in token of which we shall impart to you in a moment our paternal and affectionate apostolic blessing.

—*To Marian Congregations,* Nous sommes heureux, *September 12, 1963 (TPS)*

1. Luke 1:48.
2. Radio message to the Lisieux Marian Congress, *AAS* 53 (1961), 505-506.

Mary's Place in the Church

...The greatest spiritual joy lies in celebrating together the feast of the Assumption of Mary most holy into heaven. It is a feast that obliges us to be joyful. The other sacred commemorations dedicated to our Lady stir up our thoughtful meditation on the various moments in her earthly life and on the mysteries of her divine Son Jesus. Through them we follow her from Nazareth and Bethlehem on to Calvary, beneath the cross. We think over her worries, her hardships, her sorrows, becoming deeply engrossed in the way she is linked to the days and the sufferings of the Redeemer.

Today, on the other hand, we have to rejoice, since amid the loftiest joy we are presented with the conclusion of an exceptional and privileged life, with the bursts of glory, happiness and triumph that the Lord chose to give this most elect of creatures. We are invited to honor our Lady by echoing her *"Fecit mihi magna qui potens est,"*[1] since we too are called to join in the immense praise that the angels and saints offer her in Paradise, singing hosannas to a fullness of communion with God such as no other mere creature has ever attained.

MESSAGE OF THE "MAGNIFICAT"

And now, through this deeply-felt and indescribable participation, here we are carrying out a prophecy made by our Lady herself. We have here verification of a message that she was able to express with far-seeing vision, giving to Christian history her direction and her light. It is contained in the "Magnificat," the page of the Gospel that is proposed to us today.

"...Beatam me dicent omnes generationes." All peoples will call me blessed. What enthusiasm we have as we unite ourselves to man's processions through the ages to sing, along with Mary, of her privilege and her incomparable vocation.

WHY WE CALL MARY BLESSED

We are faced, then, with the double question of why and how we must call Mary most holy blessed. What this means is that we have to direct our attention toward the devotion that we owe to our Lady, a devotion that has taken on providential and consoling growth making it one of the most typical forms of our piety. Why—we might ask ourselves—ought I to honor our Lady this way? The answer is easy. The Lord Himself is the first one to honor her. Mary is the Mother of Christ; God's plans passed through her; in this most chosen of women Providence concentrated the hinge of its plan for the salvation of the world.

We will never be able to go deeply enough into the stupendous fact of what God has accomplished in Mary! As soon as we reflect on the special way the Lord chose to redeem the whole human family, we immediately find ourselves coming back to Mary most holy and referring to her. It would be a delightful meditation to gradually uncover God's thoughts about this lowly but great Virgin of Nazareth, who contains within herself lights and gifts and merits so outstanding that our capacity for understanding would be exhausted before we could succeed in taking the full measure of all that she presents to our intellect and to our heart.

HOW TO HONOR HER

This premise is enough to supply us with an exact answer to the second question: *how* to honor our Lady? A first fundamental of the answer is essentially connected with the wonderful relationship of light and of grace between the Almighty and the Immaculate Virgin. The immense number and variety of tributes that spring forth from the heart of the Church to celebrate Mary in worthy fashion show us very clearly the lines that ought to guide us and that certainly will not lessen our piety but will make it ever more alive.

We all recognize—and today in particular we ought to proclaim it clearly to ourselves and to others—that there is an exceptional, unique kind of devotion that we owe to Mary. The Catechism defines it as *Hyperdulia.*

BEYOND ORDINARY MEASURE

This term refers to something that goes far beyond the ordinary measure, for that would never be enough to satisfy fully our duty of veneration to Mary, for her right to such honors goes beyond any limits we might set and beyond all our capacities. And so we are face to face with a religious precept that obliges us in a very special manner.

NOT TO BE SEPARATED FROM JESUS

The second characteristic mark of this devotion and the one that gives it force comes from this basic principle: we must not separate devotion to Mary from that which we have to pay to her divine Son, Jesus our Lord. It would otherwise be like wanting to look at a lamp without paying any attention to the light that it brings with it. The lamp is beautiful if it has its light; and Mary's light is Christ, whom she bore and generated for us. If we were to disassociate Mary from Christ, devotion to Mary would lose its reason for existence. We must never separate Mary from Jesus, but rather see her dignity as coming from Christ Himself and find the reasons that make it so special precisely in the sublime honor she enjoyed of being the Mother of Christ, joined to Him through vital relationships, which is another way of saying by means of the Incarnation, the august mystery that is the starting point of our faith. So, too, we must never make her equal to Christ in our expressions of homage.

UNION, BUT TRANSCENDENCE

There are some naive minds that regard our Lady as more merciful than the Lord. Through childish judgment, they reach the conclusion that the Lord is more severe than she, and that we need to have recourse to our Lady because otherwise the Lord will punish us. It is true that our Lady is entrusted with the very special office of interceding for us, but the source of all goodness is the Lord. Christ is the one Mediator, the one font of grace. Our Lady herself is dependent upon Christ for all that she possesses. She is the *"Mater divinae gratiae"*[2] because she receives it from the Lord. And so it is absolutely necessary for us to be able to harmonize the two notions: the union of Mary with Christ, an exceptional, most fruitful, most beautiful union; and the transcendence of Christ, even with regard to Mary. This is what she herself proclaimed in her enduring song: *Fecit mihi magna qui potens est, et sanctum Nomen ejus."*[3] He that is mighty has looked down upon the humility of His handmaid: because of this, all peoples will call me blessed. Our Lady teaches us humility even and especially in the exaltation of her glory.

GUIDED BY THEOLOGY, NOT SENTIMENT

From this it follows that our devotion has to be sanctioned and guided by theology, that is, by truth; not by any kind of sentiment whatsoever, but by what God has established. Then we will see that our devotion to Mary becomes great and wonderful and, at the same time, orderly, based as it is on the overall harmony of the truths and realities that our religion presents.

Is this easy? Of course it is, especially for everyone who is docile and follows the path the Church has laid out for honoring Mary.

LIMITLESS TRUST IN MARY

And so we will have recourse to this exalted Mother with all the enthusiasm and filial love of which we are capable, and we will show her our trust in particular. Do you have trust in Mary? Do you confide in her? Do you tell her your troubles? Do you present your expectations and your hopes to her? Do you really look to her as the dispenser of goodness, of help, of kindness, of Christian friendship?

Let us think about the indescribable good fortune of being able to call her Mother, of being related to her. There is no distance between Mary and us. Instead we share the child's habit of turning to his mother at every moment and telling her everything.

In addition, it will be easy for us to honor our Lady in this way, and we will feel a keen desire to make our lives match her example as closely as possible.

Mary is our most perfect, most holy model. If we approach her with faith and tenderness, we will all but see the rays of her beauty and holiness being reflected in us. With her beside us, we will be able to be pure, good, human, meek, patient. A whole tremendous Gospel lesson of Christian living rises before us when we have such intentions as these of honoring our Lady.

PRAYER, ESPECIALLY THE ROSARY

Last of all, conversation, which means prayer. We have to pray to our Lady. Blessed are we if we are faithful in reciting that very popular and splendid prayer—the rosary—which is a kind of measured spelling out of our feelings of affection in the invocation: Hail, Mary; hail, Mary; hail, Mary. Our life will be a fortunate one if it is interwoven with this garland of roses, with this circlet of praises to Mary, to the mysteries of her divine Son! In addition to the rosary, there are other prayers to Mary that the Church places upon our lips. And so no day should ever pass without all of the faithful directing a greeting, a thought, to our Lady, thereby attracting a ray of sun and of hope upon our lives.

If we are determined and fervent in praying, we will become aware, through the very necessity of invocation, of our own extensive needs and wants. If we know how to appeal to a heart of inexhaustible goodness and mercy like Mary's, then we will make all our needs known to her and thus, you might say, take note of them in the very hope enkindled by her maternal aid. Many people do not really know themselves because they are unaware of the possibility of being cured of their misfortunes. But when we see the wonderful source of trust before us, the *Mater spei et mater veniae*,[4] then we entrust to her not only our own personal desires but those of our brothers as well, those of the world, of the Church, of the people who are working and striving so hard during these years to put the civic expression of themselves into more adequate forms.

THROUGH MARY TO CHRIST

Let us pray to our Lady to help us, to be a Mother to us; to be a Mother to the Christian people, to our families, to this parish, to our children and young people, to those who weep and who suffer. Let everyone try to bring her his own life, which may often be humble and poor, perhaps tormented, difficult, at times going astray. From our most blessed Lady he will obtain joy, light, and trust, because through her he will find Christ once again.

Are there other special intentions for more persistent prayer? Yes, many, many of them. His beloved listeners can read them in the heart of the Pope and thus become his companions in appealing to the heavenly Queen.

THE POPE'S INTENTIONS

First of all, the Church: the great family of Christians, the Mystical Body of Christ, the very family of Mary. It is urgent to obtain great aids for the Church, especially during this time of the Council, so that those who govern her may be enlightened and the Christian people may respond with ease and readiness and unselfish fervor, to put the decisions of the Council into practice.

Once again and always, pray for peace. You can see how many ups and downs the life of mankind still undergoes and how often it finds itself on the brink of a possible explosion that in erupting could bring about total ruin and destruction! You have to be justifiably anxious and vigilant in prayer, strength, and hope.

We would like to entrust another intention to you. You know that the President of the Italian Republic suddenly got much worse last night and that his condition causes deep concern. Let us raise up a special prayer for him too. Let us implore our Lady's help from Paradise for this very good and very worthy person; and may she help and protect the whole Italian populace along with the President.

Then recommend your individual families and all those who are in your minds and hearts to our Lady. It is certain that we will never look in vain for Mary's watchful care if, in keeping with the voice and the dispositions of the Church, we have always followed this incomparable Mother, if we have prayed to her, loved her, and honored her.

—Sermon in the parish church of Castel Gandolfo,
Al Vangelo, August 15, 1964 (TPS)

1. He that is mighty has done great things to me.
2. "Mother of Divine Grace."
3. He that is mighty has done great things to me and holy is his name.
4. Mother of hope and Mother of forgiveness.

New Horizons for the Woman Religious

Beloved daughters in Christ! It brings us great spiritual consolation to be able to celebrate the feast of the Nativity of Mary most holy with all you good and dear sisters!

Very often as we celebrate sacred feasts we are anxious about the understanding and the participation of the faithful present for the ceremony. We have reason to doubt whether they understand, whether they are really joining in the prayer of the Church, and whether they enjoy a full grasp of the mysteries being recalled, of the prayers being offered up, of the spiritual and moral value of all the things that worship ought to present to our souls. No such thought, no such doubt, exists now! We are sure that you are all here with us to give full meaning to this holy Mass in honor of Mary's birth, and to devote all your fervor to it. There are three obvious reasons for this that combine to make the present ceremony a solemn and memorable one.

MARY, THE DAWN OF OUR SALVATION

The first reason is that it obliges us to recall the appearance of our Lady in the world as the arrival of the dawn that comes before the light of salvation, Christ Jesus; as the opening out, on an earth covered over with the dirt of sin, of the most beautiful flower that has ever blossomed in the garden of mankind. We refer to the birth of the purest, the most innocent, the most perfect of creatures, the one most worthy of the definition that God Himself gave when creating man: image of God, likeness of God— which is to say, a beauty that is supreme, profound, so ideal in its being and form and so real in its living expression as to give us an idea of how this original creature was destined, on the one hand, to an exchange with his Creator, to the love of his Creator, in an indescribable outpouring of the most blessed and beatifying divinity and in an unconditional reply filled with poetry and joy (as the "Magnificat" of our Lady really is); and how he was destined, on the other hand, to royal dominion over the earth.

THE IMAGE OF MANKIND PERFECTED

Through a design of infinite mercy (we could almost say through a resolution for reconquest like that of the artist who, upon seeing his work shattered, decided to do it over again, and to make it even more beautiful and more in accordance with his creative idea), God took what was to appear and then disappear in miserable fashion in Eve, and He made it live again in Mary—"*ut dignum Filii tui habitaculum effici mereretur, Spiritu Sancto cooperante, praeparasti,*"[1] as the prayer you all know so well puts it. Today, a day dedicated to the veneration of this gift, of this masterpiece of God, we recall, we admire, we exult: Mary is born, Mary is ours, Mary restores to us the image of mankind perfected, in her immaculate human conception, which corresponds in a stupendous fashion to the divine mind's mysterious conception of a creature as' queen of the world.

Mary, to the fresh and supreme joy, the enchanting joy of our souls, does not hold our gaze fixed upon herself but rather urges it to look ahead, to the miracle of light and of holiness and of life that she proclaims with her birth and that she will bring with her—Christ the Lord, her son, the Son of God, from whom she herself receives everything. This is the celebrated interplay of grace that is called Incarnation and that today makes us see a presage of the coming of our salvation in Mary, the lamp that bears the divine light, the gate through which heaven will direct its steps toward earth, the mother who will offer human life to the Word of God.

You know all these things, most beloved daughters. You meditate on them, you honor them, you imitate them. Mary gives you the sublime picture of them, in which she triumphs in humility and in glory without equal. Is not this a reason to make us glad to know that all of you are intimately bound up with this joy

of the Church, with this glorification of our
Lady?

MARY'S BIRTHDAY A FAMILY EVENT

Secondly, you are celebrating this sweet
and intimate feast with us like a day in your
own home, like a family event that draws hearts
together to share in lovely sentiments. It is the
feast of everyone's heavenly Mother; and we
realize that your devotion increases by reason
of the fact that today you are celebrating it
together with this humble father of everyone on
earth, with the Pope. And the pious satisfaction
that goes with this makes us happy too, as we
feel your devotion united to our own, your
prayer to ours, your trust to ours.

We feel, dear and good Sisters, that this
morning you are the bouquet of flowers with
which we appear before Mary to express our best
wishes — or better, our devotion — on her birth-
day! A kind of childlike speech rises to our lips:
See, Mary, what we are offering you — these flowers. They are the most beautiful flowers of the
Holy Church. They are souls with a single love, a
love for your divine Son Jesus. They are souls
who have really believed His words and have
left everything to follow Him alone. They listen
to Him, they imitate Him, they serve Him, they
follow Him, along with you, yes, even to the
cross. They do not complain, they are not afraid,
they do not weep; instead they are always joyful,
they are always good, Mary, they are holy — these
daughters of the Church of Christ!

FOR RELIGIOUS, A SPECIAL PLACE
IN THE CHURCH COMMUNITY!

We hope that our most blessed Lady will listen to these simple words and that she will feel honored by the offering that we today make to her of you, sisters — indeed, of all the sisters in the Holy Church. We hope that she who is blessed among all will choose to look upon all of them with those merciful eyes of hers *("illos tuos misericordes oculos...")*, that she will choose to gladden them, that she will choose to protect and bless them; because they are hers, and they are hers because they are the Church's!

It seems to us that this meeting brings out this aspect of your religious life in a very special way. Why are you so happy to assist at the Pope's holy Mass today and to venerate our most blessed Lady along with him? And why is the Pope so happy to have you with him? Because you are, as we said, the Church's. You belong to the Mystical Body of Christ through bonds of very special adherence, and you have a special place in the Church community. You are the Church's joy, you are her honor, you are her beauty, you are her consolation, you are her example. You, we could add, are her strength! Your piety, your humility, your docility, your spirit of sacrifice make you the specially loved daughters of the holy Church.

RENEWING A "FEELING
FOR THE CHURCH"

This meeting ought to bring back to life in you a "feeling for the Church." Sometimes it happens that this "feeling for the Church" is given less attention or is less cultivated in certain religious families, by reason of the fact that they live apart and find all the objects of their immediate interest within the confines of their own communities and know little of what is going on beyond the limits of their own activities, to which they are completely dedicated. Sometimes it happens that their religious life has limited horizons, not only with regard to the course of events in this world, but even with regard to the life of the Church, her major occurrences, her thoughts and her teachings, her spiritual ardor, her sufferings and her good fortune.

This is not an ideal situation for a sister; she looses sight of the great overall vision of the divine plan for our salvation and for our sanctification. It is not a privilege to remain on the fringes of the life of the Church and to build a spirituality of your own that has nothing to do with the sharing of words, of grace and of charity that is proper to the Catholic community of the bretheren in Christ.

FULLER PARTICIPATION
IN THE LIFE OF THE CHURCH

Without depriving sisters of the silence, the recollection, the relative autonomy, and the special manner that the type of life they are leading requires, we hope that they may get back a more direct and full participation in the life of the Church, in the liturgy in particular, in social welfare, in the modern apostolate, in the service of the brethren. A great deal is being done in this direction; and we feel that it is to the benefit of the sister's sanctification and to the benefit of the faithful who are edified.

We recall that when we were at Milan, on the occasion of this very feast, we invited the dear Sisters of the Child Mary to assist at our pontifical Mass in that Duomo which is certainly one of the greatest and most beautiful cathedrals in the world, and which is dedicated to the nativity of Mary. None of those sisters had felt called through her own devotion to take part in the solemn and splendid ceremony honoring Mary's birth, a ceremony in the Cathedral of the city where they have their motherhouse as well as a magnificent network of charitable activities; the archbishop invited them. Afterward they came to the Duomo every year in large numbers. They were happy to feel that they were specially loved daughters of the Church on that day, just as we were happy to greet them during our homily and to bless them as models worthy of our approval and good will. We recall too how edifying it seemed to see, in specially reserved places in the churches of the flourishing missionary communities of southern Rhodesia and Nigeria, sisters of various religious families assisting at the Sunday services, to their great honor and to the great consolation and admiration of all the faithful.

Now then, this meeting will, we repeat, serve to re-enkindle love for the Church in you and, we hope, throughout the vast ranks of women religious. It will serve to put you in ever closer communion with her. This is a great thought—remember it—and one that can open a window onto the spiritual reality to which you have dedicated your life; the Church is the work of salvation established by Christ. It is a great thought that can comfort and sustain the modest and the hidden nature of your works; the Church is the kingdom of the Lord, and whoever belongs to it and whoever serves it shares in the dignity and fate of this kingdom. Yes, the Church is something great to think about, and the thought opens up to your generosity pathways that enable it to be ever more productive of apostolic results, wise charity, immense merits.

WOMEN AUDITORS
TO ATTEND COUNCIL

We believe that the day has come when the life of women religious has to be given greater honor and be made more effective, and that this can be done by perfecting the bonds that unite it to the life of the whole Church. We will let you in on a little secret in this regard: we have given orders that some devout qualified ladies are to attend as auditors several of the solemn ceremonies and several of the General Congregations of the coming third session of the Second Vatican Council; what we have in mind are those Congregations that will discuss matters of particular concern to the lives of women. Hence we will have present at an ecumenical council, perhaps for the first time, a representation of women — only a small one, obviously, but still significant and you might say symbolic — from you sisters, first of all, and then from the great Catholic women's organizations. Women thus will know just how much honor the Church pays to them in the dignity of their being and of their mission on the human and Christian levels.

CONCERN FOR WOMAN'S PLIGHT

While it gives us joy to let you in on this news, we are saddened by the thought of all the many aspects of modern life that portray woman as fallen from the spiritual and ethical heights attributed to her by the best civic standards and the loftiness of her Christian vocation, to the level of moral insensitivity and often of pagan license. They also show woman, in the course of having pathways of the most dangerous and harmful experiences opened to her, being deprived of the true happiness and true love that can never be separated from the sacred meaning of life.

And it pains us too to see that many feminine souls, made for lofty and generous things, today no longer know how to give their lives to full and higher meaning, because they lack two elements of interior fullness: prayer, in its complete, personal and sacramental expression; and the spirit of dedication; of a love that gives and vivifies. They remain poor and tormented souls, getting a deceptive remedy from external distractions.

THE STATE OF RELIGIOUS VOCATIONS ·

And here you have the third reason for the spiritual joy that comes to us from this meeting and brings us consolation. It is that your numbers and your fervor show that there are still strong and pure souls who have a thirst for perfection and are neither afraid nor ashamed to put on the religious habit, the habit of total consecration of one's own life to the Lord.

In truth, here again we have to make a double observation that is not a happy one. Religious vocations, for women too, are falling off; yet both the Church and secular society have a growing need for these vocations. This is one of the problems of our time for whose solution we must work and pray.

But let us linger for a moment now over the proof of religious vitality supplied by your presence here. We want to thank our Lady for this consolation, which permits us to glimpse her providential and maternal help to the Church. It offers us the example of a rebirth of Christian generosity, which makes us think of the whole treasury of good works to which your life is consecrated.

A THREEFOLD WISH

We are praying to our Lady for you, that she may give you an assurance that the choice you have made is a good one. It is the best, the most difficult and at the same time the easiest. It is the closest to that of Mary most holy because, like hers, it is completely governed by a simple and total abandonment to the divine will; *Fiat mihi secundum Verbum tuum!*[2] We will pray that she may make you strong; nowadays the religious life calls for strength. In times past it may have been a refuge for many weak and timid souls; today it is the workshop of souls that are strong, dependable, and heroic. Last of all we will pray that our Lady may make you happy and joyful. Religious life, no matter how poor and austere it may be, cannot be genuine except with interior joy! This is what we wish you as a lasting reminder of this meeting, as we ask all of you for prayers for the Council and for the whole Church, and as we give you our blessing.

— *To Women Religious*, E motivo, *September 8, 1964 (TPS)*

1. "With the help of the Holy Spirit, You have prepared her to be made a worthy dwelling place for Your Son."

2. Be it done unto me according to your word!

The Mind of the Council on Mary

This ceremony of the offering of the Candles stirs up thoughts and sentiments within us that we would like to express at greater length and leisure than that allowed us by this short interruption. We feel first of all that we owe thanks to each of you, to the Church organizations and the religious congregations and Catholic institutions you represent as you symbolically bring Catholic Rome before us in a very devoted and filial gesture of self-giving, devotion, religion, and tradition.

Your gesture has a threefold lofty meaning. It honors Christ, *"lumen ad revelationem gentium,"* light to enlighten the nations[1]; it pays tribute to Mary, the Mother of the Word made man, with an act of devotion that links us with the oldest and most venerable Eastern and Latin liturgies; and it shows the Pope how Rome is united to him as her father and bishop in a faithful and heartfelt fashion. Thank you, beloved brothers and sons! May the gifts and sentiments of which you bring us such noble evidence and comforting consolation prove spiritually rewarding to you and those you represent.

TRADITIONAL ROMAN PIETY

How wonderful it would be to dig more deeply into this awareness of abundant and stirring religious, historical and ecclesial values! How fruitful it would be in lofty reflections if we were to consider along with you the look of Roman piety, one that is unknown to many people and is nowadays hidden over by the modern aspect of the city, itself very respectable and dear and yet unfortunately somewhat forgetful of the sacred lines of its ancient, fascinating religious image, and not always as proud as it should be of the extraordinary treasures of art, archaeology, and devotion that adorn its regal "form" like no other city in the world. Along with a kind of transparent vision of the centuries and the places of our Christian Rome, you are offering us a sacred continuation of the matchless spirituality that comes from her history of teaching nations and saints her indescribable art of believing and praying. You bring us wonderful consolation by showing us through actions that speak and through faithful hearts that history is not just a dream of times laid to rest, nor just a legendary piece of poetry disengaged from the prose of current materialistic reality, but rather a song that continues, a voice that is still alive and intoning a new verse that may now be fuller and more sonorous than ever before—a voice of conscience, of culture, of tormented and passionate love.

We want to congratulate you today for this: for the persistency, indeed the revival, of Roman devotion. It gives us immense pleasure to see that this devotion is the happy and jealous heir to the liturgical treasures of a tradition that is authoritative and papal as well as popular and spontaneous, and to see that, in you, it is eager to revive its religious spirit with new and authentic expressions, such as those prescribed by the recent Constitution on the Sacred Liturgy.[2]

ROME'S LOYALTY TO MARY

We want our congratulations and our recommendations to lay stress on one point, the very one that we are illustrating at this moment in this ceremony, namely, devotion to Mary most holy. We are very glad about the wealth, the beauty, and the fullness that this Rome of ours has always — and no less today — reserved for our Lady in its monuments, in the liturgy, in the devotion of faithful hearts. We are convinced that a fountain of blessings is linked to this loyalty to Marian devotion — such blessings as adherence to the true faith of our Lord Jesus Christ, affection for His Gospel, efforts at Christian regeneration of morals and of feeling, pride and joy in belonging to the Catholic Church, profound trust in her maternal protection that is capable of instilling into souls the strongest of moral energies and the gentlest of spiritual consolations.

MARIAN DOGMA A KIND OF SYNTHESIS

Blessed are we, brethren and sons, for we have been trained in this devotion to the Mother of Christ in the school of the holy Church. Through a kind of incontrovertible experience, we feel how this devotion that we want to be profound, personal, human, and truly tender, does not in any way separate us from the recognition of the unique, transcendent, divine font of truth, life, and grace that is Christ Jesus. Instead, it leads us to Him, binds us to Him, unites us to Him, as the one who alone is holy, the one who alone is Lord, the one who alone is our most high Teacher and our Redeemer. We feel, indeed, that the teaching on Mary and Marian devotion introduce us into the plan of salvation that Christ has established—in the sense that, as has been so well said, there is in Marian dogma a "symbolic summary of the Catholic doctrine on human cooperation in the redemption; in this way, it offers a kind of synthesis of the very dogma on the Church." [3]

HOMAGE TO THE MOTHER OF THE CHURCH

Shouldn't we feel glad that our attention was recently directed to this genuine doctrine and worship through the authoritative, beautiful, profound, and exact statement made by the Ecumenical Council when it wisely inserted the chapter on the Blessed Virgin Mary into the monumental Constitution on the Church? And won't we give the title of "Mother of the Church"—one that we recognized as due Mary most holy at this very moment of the maturing of the doctrine on the Church—the meaning of Mother of Christians, our spiritual Mother because she is the natural Mother of Christ, our Head and our Redeemer? As has been equally well said, under one aspect the Blessed Virgin is a part, a daughter of the Church, our sister, because like us, although in an eminent and privileged way, she too has been redeemed by Christ; but under another aspect, because she is the one who generated the Son of God made man, she is the *"Theotokos,"* the Mother of God, Queen of the Church, Mother of the Mystical Body according to faith and charity. "If devotion is, for the most part, directed toward the individual aspects of Mary's spiritual maternity, is it not perhaps desirable to have this view completed by its community aspect and to have the attention of the faithful called to this?"

THE UPCOMING MARIAN CONGRESS IN SANTO DOMINGO

These ties of Mary with the Church, and many others as well (like the one dear to St. Ambrose — *Ecclesiae typus* [5] — in Luke 2:7), along with other doctrinal matter dealing with our Lady, will certainly be the object of meditation, publicity, and celebration at the approaching International Marian Congress, scheduled for Santo Domingo at the end of March. We want to express the wish that along with our Cardinal Legate there will be a great number of bishops, priests and faithful who will come with great fervor from every part of the world and especially from America to pay tribute to

Mary most holy, and to impress upon the devotion and piety with which we want to honor her that Christocentric and ecclesiological orientation that the Council intended to give to our Marian doctrine and devotion.

ITS POST-CONCILIAR AND RENOVATING CHARACTER

We feel sure that this orientation, which sets her who was "blessed among women" in her loftiest and truest splendor, will impress upon the Congress a character that is post-conciliar, renovating, and a guiding force in promoting Catholic devotion to Mary. We feel sure that it will give it the merit of seeking out the true and faithful sources of the devotion itself in the pages of Sacred Scripture, in the teachings of the Fathers, in the speculations of the Masters, and in the traditional doctrine of the Church, Eastern as well as Latin, in such a way that study by Catholics of the Mother of Christ and devotion to her will result in the added benefit of bringing together around Mary, "*Mater unitatis*,"[6] not only all the Catholics who are already close to her as children in so many different ways, but, God willing, all Christians as well, including those still separated from us. For, if they are not already enjoying it, a great joy is being prepared that will come to them on the day when they are integrated into the one Church founded and willed by

Christ. It is the joy of rediscovering Mary, who is humble and most exalted in the essential role God assigned to her in the plan of our salvation.

And so we think that this post-conciliar Congress, and along with it devotion to Mary throughout the world, will turn toward a deepening of understanding and love for the mysteries of Mary, rather than toward a dialectical effort at theological speculations that are still questionable and are more likely to divide individuals than to unite them. It will stir up ever more attentive and admiring reflection upon the content of truth that is at the root of devotion to Mary, tempering, where need be, any sentimentalism of an unbalanced or unenlightened nature that may have sprung up around it. What this means is that it will encourage a serious and living devotion to our Lady, the devotion that is to be found at work in the great and unified liturgical plan of the Church, calling the faithful back to a profession of true love and to a practice of true imitation with regard to the Blessed Virgin—a love and imitation that will show more and more the immense spiritual and moral value of devotion to Mary.

These are the wishes that we can apply to ourselves in order to honor our Lady in a worthy fashion on this feast of hers and in order to enjoy the good fortune of her maternal protection and her heavenly blessings. And may our apostolic blessing now serve to assure you of them, beloved sons.

FACTORS IN DISTRIBUTING THE CANDLES

Now, we imagine that you would like to know what destination we have chosen, in keeping with a nice and meaningful custom introduced a few years ago, for these candles that have been blessed on the feast of the Purification of Mary most holy. It is a gesture with profound symbolism which fits in very well with the mysterious richness of today's splendid liturgy. Just as in other years, we want it to be a kind of heartfelt suggestion that applies to the present moment in the life of the Church and that will be indicative of the aims and intentions and feelings that occupy our mind after the unforgettable experiences of last year.

DESTINATIONS ANNOUNCED

We will destine the candles that you have given us, first, in keeping with custom, to the new diplomatic representatives of various countries recently accredited to the Holy See, and next to the twenty-seven new Cardinals whom we have just called to become part of the Senate of the Church; then to the Catholic universities, which are holding aloft in the world the prestige of culture strengthened by faith; to the churches and institutions of Bombay, along with the distinguished president of the noble Indian nation, as a renewed pledge of our gratitude for the welcome extended to our pilgrimage last December; to our brethren in the episcopate who concelebrated the' divine Sacrifice with us at the close of the third session of the Second Vatican Ecumenical Council; to the churches in the Vajont region, rising again from the ruins; to the missionary institutes of men and women that have suffered so much from recent sad events in various parts of the world; and to the prefectures of our diocese of Rome, as testimony to our gratitude.

May these candles serve to carry an announcement of joy and of evangelical peace into every place, and along with it an outpouring of our paternal affection, and our blessing.

— On the feast of the Purification,
La cerimonia dell'offerta, February 2, 1965 (TPS)

1. Lk. 2:32.
2. Cf. *TPS* IX, 316-338 — Ed.
3. De Lubac, *Méditationes sur l'Église*, p. 242.
4. Galot, *Nouvelle Revue Théologique*, December, 1964, p. 1180-1.
5. Type of Church.

Christi Matri

*To His Venerable Brothers the Patriarchs,
Primates, Archbishops, Bishops and
Other Local Ordinaries in Peace and
Communion with the Apostolic See:*
enjoining prayers to the Blessed Virgin Mary
during October

Venerable brothers, health and apostolic benediction.

It is a solemn custom of the faithful during the month of October to weave the prayers of the rosary into mystical garlands for the Mother of Christ. Following in the footsteps of our predecessors, we heartily approve this, and we call upon all the sons of the Church to offer special devotions to the most blessed Virgin this year. For the danger of a more serious and extensive calamity hangs over the human family and has increased, especially in parts of eastern Asia where a bloody and hard-fought war is raging. So we feel most urgently that we must once again do what we can to safeguard peace. We are also disturbed by what we know to be going on in other areas, such as the growing nuclear armaments race, the senseless nationalism, the racism, the obsession for revolution, the separations imposed upon citizens, the nefarious plots, the slaughter of innocent people. All of these can furnish material for the greatest calamity.

A SPECIAL TASK FROM GOD

Like our immediate predecessors, we seem to have received a special task from God in His Providence to work patiently and constantly to preserve and strengthen peace. This task, as is evident, arises from the fact that we have been entrusted with the governing of the whole Church, which, as a "sign lifted up to the nations,"[1] does not serve political ends but rather must bring the truth and grace of Jesus Christ, its divine Founder, to mankind.

Indeed, from the very beginning of our apostolic ministry, we have omitted no effort to further the cause of peace in the world through prayers, entreaties and exhortations. As you well remember, last year we flew to North America to speak about the most desirable blessing of peace at the General Assembly of the United Nations, before a very distinguished audience representing almost every nation.[2] We warned against allowing some to be inferior to others, and against allowing some to attack others. Instead, all should devote their efforts and zeal to the establishment of peace. Even afterwards, moved by apostolic concern, we did not stop urging those upon whom this great matter depends to ward off from mankind the frightful disaster that might result.

A VERY GRAVE OBLIGATION

Now once again we raise our voice "with a loud cry and with tears,"[3] urgently beseeching those who rule over nations to do everything they can to see to it that the conflagration spreads no farther but rather is completely extinguished. We do not doubt that all men who want what is right and honorable—whatever their race, color, religion and social class—feel the same as we do.

Therefore, let all those responsible bring about the necessary conditions for the laying down of arms before the possibility of doing so is taken away by the pressure of events. Those in whose hands rests the safety of the human race should realize that in this day and age they have a very grave obligation in conscience. Mindful of their own nation, of the world, of God and history, let them examine their own consciences. Let them realize that in the future their names will be blessed if they wisely succeed in complying with this exhortation.

NEGOTIATIONS MUST BEGIN

In the name of the Lord we cry out to them to stop. Men must come together and get down to sincere negotiations. Things must be settled now, even at the cost of some loss or inconvenience, for later they may have to be settled at the cost of immense harm and enormous slaughter that cannot even be imagined now. But this peace must be based on justice and freedom for mankind, and must take into account the rights of individuals and communities. Otherwise it will be fluid and unstable.

As we say all this with deep emotion and an anxious heart, it is only right for us to do as our supreme pastoral care urges, and ask for help from heaven. Peace, which "is such a great good that even among earthly, mortal things, there is nothing more pleasant to hear, nothing more ardently desired, and finally nothing better to be found," [4] has to be sought from Him who is the Prince of Peace. [5] But since the Church, in uncertain and anxious times, has been accustomed to have recourse to that most ready intercessor, her Mother Mary, we have good reason to direct our own attention and yours, venerable brethren, and that of all the Christian faithful, to her. For as St. Irenaeus says, she "has become the cause of salvation for the whole human race." [6]

MARY, QUEEN OF PEACE

Nothing seems more appropriate and valuable to us than to have the prayers of the whole Christian family rise to the Mother of God, who is invoked as the Queen of Peace, begging her to pour forth abundant gifts of her maternal goodness in the midst of so many great trials and hardships. We want constant and devout prayers to be offered to her whom we declared Mother of the Church, its spiritual parent, during the celebration of the Second Vatican Council, thereby winning the applause of the Fathers and of the Catholic world, and confirming a point of traditional doctrine. For the Mother of the Savior is, as St. Augustine teaches, "surely the mother of His members,"[7] and St. Anselm, to mention only one other, agrees with him in these words: "What could ever be deemed more suitable than for you to be the mother of those whose father and brother Christ deigned to become?"[8] She was called "most truly the Mother of the Church" by our predecessor Leo XIII.[9] Hence we have good reason to place our trust in her in the midst of this terrible disorder.

THE VALUE OF THE ROSARY

If evils increase, the devotion of the People of God should also increase. And so, venerable brothers, we want you to take the lead in urging and encouraging people to pray ardently to our most merciful mother Mary by saying the rosary during the month of October, as we have already indicated. This prayer is well suited to the devotion of the People of God, most pleasing to the Mother of God and most effective in gaining heaven's blessings. The Second Vatican Council recommended use of the rosary to all the sons of the Church, not in express words but in unmistakable fashion in this phrase: "Let them value highly the pious practices and exercises directed to the Blessed Virgin and approved over the centuries by the magisterium."[10]

As the history of the Church makes clear, this very fruitful way of praying is not only efficacious in warding off evils and preventing calamities, but is also of great help in fostering Christian life. "It nourishes the Catholic faith which readily takes on new life from a timely commentary on the sacred mysteries, and it turns minds towards the truths that have been taught us by God." [11]

OCTOBER 4th OBSERVANCE

And so during the month of October, dedicated to Our Lady of the Rosary, prayers and petitions should be increased, so that through her intercession the dawn of true peace may shine forth to men. This means true religious peace too, for unfortunately, not everyone is allowed to profess his religion freely in this age. In particular, we want October 4th—the day on which, as we mentioned earlier, we went last year to the United Nations for the sake of peace—to be celebrated throughout the whole Catholic world this year as a Day of Prayer for Peace. It will be up to you, venerable brethren, in the light of your own commendable devotion and on the basis of the obvious importance of this matter, to prescribe sacred ceremonies in which priests, religious and the faithful—especially boys and girls in the flower of their innocence, and the sick and others who are suffering—can all ask the help of the Mother of God and of the Church.

On that day we ourself will go to St. Peter's Basilica, to the tomb of the Prince of the Aposties, to offer special prayers to the Virgin Mother of God, protector of Christians and mediator for peace. In this way heaven will be moved, in a sense, by the one voice of the Church resounding from all the continents on the earth. For as St. Augustine says, "Amid the various languages of men, the faith of the heart speaks one tongue." [12]

AN APPEAL TO MARY

Look down with maternal clemency, most Blessed Virgin, upon all your children. Consider the anxiety of bishops who fear that their flocks will be tormented by a terrible storm of evils. Heed the anguish of so many people, fathers and mothers of families who are uncertain about their future and beset by hardships and cares. Soothe the minds of those at war and inspire them with "thoughts of peace." Through your intercession, may God, the avenger of injuries, turn to mercy. May He give back to nations the tranquility they seek and bring them to a lasting age of genuine prosperity.

With confidence that the exalted Mother of God will graciously hear our humble prayer, we lovingly impart the apostolic blessing to you, venerable brethren, and to the clergy and people committed to your care.

Given at St. Peter's, Rome, on the 15th day of September, in the year 1966, the fourth of our pontificate.

—Encyclical Letter, Christi Matri, September, 1966 (TPS)

Prayer Intentions at Fatima

Great is our desire to honor the Blessed Virgin Mary, Christ's Mother and therefore the Mother of God. Great is our confidence in her benevolence toward the holy Church and toward our apostolic mission. Great is our need for her intercession with Christ, her divine Son. For these reasons we have come as a lowly and trustful pilgrim to this blessed sanctuary. Here today we are celebrating the 50th anniversary of the apparitions at Fatima, and the 25th anniversary of the consecration of the world to the Immaculate Heart of Mary.

CONCERN FOR ALL MEN

It is a pleasure to be here with you, beloved brothers and sons, to join with you in professing our devotion to Mary, to associate you with our prayer. In this way our common veneration may be more public and more filial, and our plea may gain more ready acceptance.

We extend a greeting to all of you here present—in particular, to the citizens of this illustrious nation which in its long history has given the Church many great and holy men and a pious, hard-working people. We greet all you pilgrims who have come from near and far, and all the members of the Catholic Church in Rome and around the world who are spiritually present at this altar with us. Greetings to you all. We are here to celebrate Holy Mass with you and for you. We are united together here, as children of one family, around our heavenly Mother, so that during the Holy Sacrifice we may achieve closer and more salvific communion with Christ, our Lord and Savior.

We do not want to exclude anyone from this spiritual remembrance, because it is our wish that everyone share in the graces we are now going to implore from heaven. All of you have a place in our heart: our brother bishops, priests, men and women religious who have consecrated yourselves to Christ in total love; all Christian families; all you beloved lay people who wish to join forces with the clergy in extending the kingdom of God; all you young people and children whom we always want to have near us; all you who are weary and afflicted, all you who weep and suffer hardship, knowing full well that Christ calls you to His side to associate you with His redeeming passion and to give you comfort.

Our gaze turns also to all Christians who are not Catholics but who are our brothers through Baptism. We mention them with the hope of full communion with them in the unity that the Lord desires. And we also turn to the whole world. We do not want to set any limits to our love; in this moment we extend it to all mankind, to every government and to every nation of the earth.

PRAYER FOR THE CHURCH

You are aware of the special intentions which we wish to make the emblem of this pilgrimage. We shall recall them here, so that they may inspire our prayer and enlighten all who are listening to us.

The first intention is the Church: the one, holy, catholic and apostolic Church. As we have said, we wish to pray for its internal peace. The Ecumenical Council awakened many energies within the Church. It opened up broader perspectives in the whole area of Church doctrine. It has called all the Church's sons to a clearer awareness, a closer collaboration, and a more active apostolate. We earnestly hope that this beneficial and profound renewal will be carried on and further developed.

POTENTIALLY DISRUPTIVE ENERGIES

What a shame it would be if some arbitrary interpretation, not authorized by the Church's magisterium, were to turn this spiritual renewal into a disruptive force which would undermine the Church's traditional constitutional structure a force which would replace the theology of the great authentic teachers with new partisan ideologies that would try to exclude from the norm of faith everything which modern thought — often lacking the light of reason — does not understand and accept; a force which would convert the apostolic concern of redeeming charity into base acquiescence to the negative qualities of the secular mentality and the way of the world. Our attempt to draw all men together would be a vain effort indeed if the Church did not offer, to our separated Christian brothers and to the rest of humanity who are not of our faith, the patrimony of truth and charity in its full authenticity and its original splendor — the patrimony which the Church guards and distributes.

We want to pray to Mary for a living Church, an authentic Church, a united Church, a holy Church. We wish to pray together with you that the hopes and energies aroused by the Council may bring us an abundant outpouring of the fruits of the Holy Spirit. He is the source of an authentic Christian life and we celebrate His feast tomorrow, the day of Pentecost. His fruits are listed by St. Paul: "charity, joy, peace, patience, kindness, goodness, faith, modesty, continency" (Gal. 5:22-23).

It is our desire to offer a prayer that worship of God will maintain its priority in the world, today and forever; that His law will shape the conscience and the conduct of modern man. Faith in God is humanity's guiding light, and it should not be extinguished in the hearts of men. On the contrary, it should burn brighter under the stimulus provided by science and progress.

This line of thought motivates and animates our prayer, but in this moment it also makes us think of those countries where religious freedom is, for all practical purposes, suppressed; where rejection of God is fostered as if it represented the truth of a new age and the liberation of the populace. The truth is quite different, however. Let us pray for these nations. Let us pray for our fellow believers in these countries, that God's inner power may sustain them and that genuine civil liberty may be granted to them.

PRAYER FOR PEACE

Now let us move on to the second intention that motivates this pilgrimage: the world, world peace. As you know, since the Council there has been a growing awareness of the Church's mission to the world, her mission of service and love. You know that the world is at a stage where great transformations are taking place, where enormous and wondrous progress is being made, where the riches of the earth and of the universe are being discovered and tapped. Yet you also can see that the world is not happy or tranquil.

WORLD IN DANGER

The first cause of this unrest resides in the fact that it is difficult to establish harmony, to insure peace. Everything seems to push the world toward brotherhood and unity; and yet we find terrifying and unabating conflicts in the heart of humanity. Humanity's present situation in history is made critical by two principal factors: man possesses a huge arsenal of frighteningly lethal weapons, but his moral progress does not keep pace with his scientific and technical progress. Furthermore, a large part of humanity is still enmeshed in hunger and poverty, while at the same time it experiences a growing and discomforting awareness of its own needs and of the prosperity of others. That is why we say that the world is in danger. That is why we have come to the feet of the Queen of Peace to plead for peace, the gift which only God can grant us.

AN APPEAL TO ALL MEN

Yes, peace is a gift from God. It requires His beneficial, merciful and mysterious intervention. But His gift is not always a miraculous one. It is a gift which works its wonders in the recesses of men's hearts, and hence it is a gift requiring ready acceptance and cooperation on our part. And so, after directing our prayer to heaven, we direct it to men all over the world. In this singular moment we say to them: Prove yourselves worthy of God's gift of peace! Be truly men! Be good, be prudent! Open your hearts and give thought to the good of the whole world! Be generous! Try to see that your prestige and interests are not opposed to those of others, but rather are one with theirs! Do not dwell upon schemes of destruction and death, of violence and revolution! Think rather about projects of mutual aid and joint collaboration!

Men of the world, consider the gravity and the grandeur of this moment, which could well be decisive for this generation and the generations to come! Begin again to draw together with the intention of building a new world, a world of real human beings, which cannot be fashioned unless God is the sun that shines on its horizon. Hear in our lowly and tremulous voice the echo of Christ's own words: "Blessed are the meek, for they shall possess the earth; blessed are the peacemakers for they shall be called children of God."

You can see, dear sons and brothers listening to us, the drama and awesomeness that surround the world and its fortunes, as we have pictured it. It is a panorama which our Lady opens up to us, a scene which we contemplate with frightened but ever trustful eyes. It is a scene that we shall always approach as our Lady told us to approach it—with prayer and penance. That we pledge! May it record no more incidents of conflict, tragedy and catastrophe, but rather the conquests made by love and the victories won by peace.

—At the 50th Anniversary Celebration of the Fatima Apparitions, Tão grande é, May 13, 1967 (TPS)

A Schoolboy Memory
of Our Lady

A memory of times long past, of our life as a schoolboy, brings back to mind a building overlooking the old school courtyard, surmounted by a statue of our Lady. At the foot of the statue was an inscription in large letters: "Look down from on high on your children." The inscription was always before us as we looked at the facade of that beautiful building, beneath which we played and got ready for school and for life.

War has destroyed the house, and must have changed everything. But our memory still has engraved in it that short inscription, dedicated to Mary, placed with the sky as its background, and addressed to us boys, who were being initiated into our studies and into the experience of the years to come. It returns to our memory today, as the best wish of this feast which unites heaven and earth – a wish for you, dearly beloved children gathered here, and for all who hear our voice and the affectionate expression of our soul.

Yes, Mary, called to share the heavenly glory of her Son, the risen Jesus Christ, our Savior, surely still "looks down from on high on her children." In this consoling certainty we invoke her today for all who are indeed spiritually her sons: for all Christians, for the whole Church, of which we gave her the title, in the recent Council, of Mother—mystical "Mother of the Church," Mother of Christ's Mystical Body as she was the natural Mother of His physical body, the body in which took place the Incarnation of the Word of God, and the Redemption of the world.

We call on her for peace on the earth that is still stained with blood and hatred among men who are brothers; we call on her for justice in human society, for the sanctification of all; and we repeat: "Mary, look down from on high on your children."

—Angelus message, August 15, 1969 (TPS)

Praying the Rosary for Peace

The recurrence of the month of October provides us with an occasion for inviting the entire Christian people once more to the practice of the form of prayer which is rightly dear to Catholic piety, and which has lost none of its importance amid the difficulties of the present day. We are speaking of the rosary of the Blessed Virgin Mary.

MISUNDERSTANDINGS PREVALENT

The intention which we would propose this year to all our sons and daughters, since it seems to us more serious and urgent than ever, is that of peace among men and between peoples. Despite some progress and some legitimate hopes, murderous conflicts are continuing, new points of tension are appearing, and even Christians, who appeal to the same Gospel of love, are seen to be in opposition to one another. Within the Church itself, misunderstandings arise between brothers who mutually accuse and condemn each other. Hence it is more urgent than ever to work and pray for peace.

An anniversary increases our confidence
in this effort, namely, the fourth centenary of
the apostolic bull *Consueverunt Romani Pontifices,*[1] by which St. Pius V gave the rosary a
form suitable for all time, during a period of
many troubles for both the Church and the world.
Faithful to this sacred heritage, from which the
Christian people have never ceased to draw
strength and courage, we exhort the clergy
and faithful to beg earnestly from God, through
the intercession of the Virgin Mary, peace and
reconciliation among all men and between
all peoples.

I. The Intercession of Mary

Undoubtedly, peace is the concern of men
and a good common to all. As such, it must be
the constant care of everyone, but especially of
those who carry the responsibility of states and
of the community of peoples. But indeed, who
does not have a share of responsibility in the
life and peace of a family, of an enterprise, of
an association? Despite much good will, there
are many interests in opposition; much selfishness is shown; many antagonisms increase;
many rivalries conflict with one another. Who
does not see, then, the unflagging action de-
manded from each and all in order that love
may triumph over discord, and that peace may
be restored to the city of men?

NO PEACE WITHOUT GOD

But peace is also the concern of God. He
has placed in our hearts the ardent desire for

peace. He urges us to work toward it, each doing his share, and for that purpose He sustains our feeble energies and our vacillating wills. He alone can give us a peaceful soul, and confirm in depth and solidity our efforts for peace.

Prayer, by which we ask for the gift of peace, is therefore an irreplaceable contribution to the establishment of peace. It is through Christ, in whom all grace is given us,[2] that we dispose ourselves to welcome the gift of peace. And in that undertaking, how can we do otherwise than to depend lovingly upon the incomparable intercession of Mary, His Mother, of whom the Gospel tells us that she "found favor with God"?[3]

REASONS FOR CONFIDENCE

It is the humble Virgin of Nazareth who became Mother of "the Prince of Peace,"[4] of Him who was born under the sign of peace,[5] and who proclaimed to the whole world: "Blessed are the peacemakers, for they shall be called sons of God."[6] The Gospel teaches us that Mary is sensitive to the needs of men. At Cana, she did not hesitate to intervene, to the joy of the villagers invited to a wedding feast.[7] How, then, would she not intervene in favor of peace, that precious possession, if we only pray to her with a sincere heart?

The Second Vatican Ecumenical Council reminds us most opportunely that Mary continues to intercede with her Son in favor of her children on earth.[8] When she quite simply told Him, "They have no wine," Christ responded most generously. How, then, would He not show the same generosity to her when she says, "They have no peace"?

II. Obligation of Every Christian

If every man, "as much as he can, as best he can," [9] must work for justice and peace in the world, then each Christian will have it at heart to ask Mary to pray with us and for us, so that that peace which the Lord alone can give, may be granted us.[10] Moreover, by meditating upon the mysteries of the most holy rosary we learn, through Mary's example, to become peaceful souls, through loving and unceasing association with Jesus and with the mysteries of His redemptive life.

ALL MUST PRAY

Let all the children of the holy Church pray:

—*Children and young people,* whose future is at stake amid the changes that are shaking the world. Let parents, teachers and all priests strive to make of them men consecrated to prayer.

—*The ill and the elderly,* who sometimes are disheartened by their seeming uselessness. They should rediscover the powerful strength of prayer, and become loving souls, drawing men peacefully toward the source of peace.

— *Adults,* who work hard all day long. They will find their efforts bearing more fruit when these arise from a life of prayer.[11] By knowing Mary they will the better know and love Jesus. Many of our ancestors in the faith have had this life-giving experience.

— *Consecrated souls,* whose life, like Mary's, must always be closely bound to the life of Christ, so as to irradiate His message of love and peace.

— *Bishops and their priestly assistants,* who have the special mission of praying "in the name of the Church on behalf of the whole people entrusted to them and indeed for the whole world."[12] In the depths of their prayer, they will surely unite themselves with the supplication of Mary.

In this ardent desire for peace, which is the "fruit of the Spirit,"[13] we shall all devote ourselves, like the apostles in the upper room, "to prayer together with... Mary the mother of Jesus."[14]

III. Prayer Intentions

We shall pray for all who perform the tasks of peace in the world, from the humblest village to the greatest international organizations. Together with our encouragement and our gratitude, they have a right also to our prayers. "How beautiful upon the mountains are the feet of him who brings good tidings, who publishes peace, who brings good tidings of good, who publishes salvation."[15]

We shall pray that everywhere there may be vocations to become doers of peace, workers for concord and for reconciliation between men and among peoples. We shall pray that in every heart, starting with our own, sectarianism and racism, hatred and wickedness, may be rooted out, since they are the ever-recurring source of wars and divisions. For if evil is strong, grace is even stronger.

We shall pray to Him who died for our sins "to gather into one the children of God who are scattered abroad." [16] We shall pray that among all the sons and daughters of the Church there may be a climate of mutual respect and confidence, of dialogue and reciprocal benevolence. We shall pray that all, while recognizing their differences, may realize that they complement one another, in the truth and love of Christ, according to the recommendation of the great Apostle St. Paul: "So far as it depends upon you, live peaceably with all.... Let us no more pass judgment on one another.... The kingdom of God...[means] righteousness and peace and joy in the Holy Spirit.... Let us then pursue what makes for peace and for mutual upbuilding." [17]

ALL MUST BE PEACEMAKERS

We ourself, honored brothers, beloved sons and daughters, shall never cease to labor and pray for peace, as the vicar of Him who "is our peace...making peace...bringing the hostility to an end." [18] With the Apostle Paul, under whose name we would conceal our littleness, we exhort you "to lead a life worthy of the calling to which you have been called, with all lowliness and meekness, with patience, forbearing one another in love, eager to maintain the unity of the Spirit in the bond of peace." [19]

May the frequent meditation upon the mysteries of our salvation make you peacemakers, in the image of Christ, after the example of Mary. May the rosary, in the form handed down by St. Pius V — as well as in other recent forms adapting it, with the consent of the lawful authority, to the needs of today — be indeed, as our beloved predecessor Pope John XXIII desired, "a great public and universal prayer for the ordinary and extraordinary needs of the holy Church, of the nations, and of the entire world," [20] for this rosary is, as it were, "the Gospel in miniature," [21] and "henceforth, a devotion of the Church." [22]

By this prayer to Mary, the most holy Mother of God and our Mother, we help to realize the wish of the Council: "Let all faithful Christians offer urgent prayers to the Mother of God and Mother of men in order that she may intercede with her Son in the communion of all the saints, until the whole family of nations — whether they bear the honored name of Christian or still do not know their Savior — may be joyfully assembled into a single People of God, in peace and harmony, to the glory of the most holy and undivided Trinity." [23]

It is with this intention, honored brothers, beloved sons and daughters, that we bestow upon you with all our heart our apostolic blessing, inviting you to recite the holy rosary with fervor during this month of October.

Given at Rome, at St. Peter's, October 7, in the year 1969, the seventh of our pontificate.

—Apostolic Exhortation, Recurrens Mensis October, October, 1969 (TPS)

1. *Bull. Ord. Praed.*, Sept. 17, 1569, vol. V, p. 223.
2. See Rom. 8:32.
3. Lk. 1:30.
4. Is. 9:5.
5. See Lk. 2:14.
6. Mt. 5:9.
7. See Jn. 2:15.
8. See *Dogmatic Constitution on the Church*, no. 62: *AAS* 57 (1965), 63 (*TPS* X, 397-398).
9. See encyc. *Populorum Progressio*, no. 75: *AAS* 59 (1967), 294 (*TPS* XII, 168).
10. See Collect of the Mass for Peace.
11. See *Dogmatic Constitution on the Church*, no. 34: *AAS* 57 (1965), 39-40 (*TPS* X, 382).
12. *Degree on the Priestly Ministry and Life*, no. 5: *AAS* 58 (1966), 998.
13. Gal. 5:22.
14. Acts 1:14.
15. Is. 52:7.
16. See Jn. 11:52.
17. Rom. 12:18 and 14, 13, 17, 19.
18. Eph. 2:14-16.
19. *Ibid.*, 4:1-3.
20. Apostolic letter *Il religioso convegno*, Sept. 29, 1961: *AAS* 53 (1961), 646.
21. Cardinal J. G. Saliége, *Voilà ta Mère* (Marian pages assembled and presented by Msgr. Garrone), Toulouse: Apostolat de la prière (1958), p. 40.
22. Paul VI, allocution to participants in 3rd International Dominican Rosary Congress, July 13, 1963: *Insegnamenti di Paolo VI*, I (1963), 464.
23. *Dogmatic Constitution on the Church*, no. 69: *AAS* 57 (1965), 66-67 (*TPS* X, 399-400).

The Right Use of Prayer

...We need our Lady's help. A tormented, famous spiritual and realistic writer, Charles Peguy, compared the "Our Father" and "Hail Mary" of the rosary to ships sailing victoriously toward the Father. We too should attempt that mystic voyage. Do not let it be said that by doing so we are "using" prayer and devotion to our Lady for our own temporal desires; that this sort of religion is just utilitarianism, the same that pervades modern life at all points. To begin with, there is nothing wrong in making prayer a confession of our limitations, of our needs, and of our trust in being able to obtain from on high what our own powers are unable to obtain. Did not Christ Himself teach us to do this? Did He not say, "Ask, and it shall be given to you; seek, and you shall find; knock, and it shall be opened to you"?...

—General Audience, October 8, 1969 (TPS)

Lessons from Mary
for the Synod

Surely none of us is surprised to find himself at this stational church, the Basilica of St. Mary Major, during the extraordinary Synod of Bishops. The basilica is a venerable sanctuary of Marian devotion, and dear to the heart of Rome. Indeed, each of us probably feels welling up within himself a spontaneous need to express his full devotion to Mary at this time. It is a moment when reflection on our vocation of belonging to the Mystical Body of Christ, which is the Church, invites us to recall and honor the woman who was the Blessed Mother of the physical body of the Son of God, who thus became the Son of Man.[1]

We who are vested with Christ's priesthood have an avid desire to justify Catholic devotion to Mary, to debate and dispute those who impugn the legitimacy of this devotion or seek to minimize it. We may earnestly seek to bring out the biblical, theological, traditional and affective claims that give shape to this devotion. But in so doing, we may sometimes allow our own vital and filial expression of devotion to her to languish a bit, finding it harder today to make time for heartfelt conversation with her, who is Christ's Mother according to the flesh and thereby spiritually our mother, the Mother of the Church.

But note that we who came together to participate in the Synod, or to follow its unfolding ceremonies and the themes of common interest, have felt in our hearts a happy impulse, which now leads us to conclude the synodal assembly near Mary and under her maternal gaze.

MARY AND THE CHURCH

Once again we have been deliberating on the Church, on its essential trait of hierarchical communion, on the mysterious reality of the generative power conferred on certain chosen ministers of the People of God. And in doing this, we have noticed once again the relationship that exists between Mary and the Church, and especially her relationship to those Church members who have particular functions in the Church. We refer to priests and pastors of souls, who are commissioned to proclaim the Word of God in the ministry of preaching, to pour out the life-giving and sanctifying Spirit in the sacraments, and to provide pastoral direction to the faithful on their journey through time and eternity. It is because of her relationship to us that we are gathered here this evening.

We find here a relationship by analogy. Mary is the Mother of Christ; the Church is the mother of Christians. The more evident this aspect of the Church becomes, the more clearly the mystery of the Incarnation, from its epiphany in Bethlehem, is reflected down through history in every local church and in the Church of Rome — particularly in this basilica called "the Bethlehem of Rome" — so much easier and more obligatory becomes the comparison, the relationship between Mary and the Church.

MYSTICAL PARALLELS

Here let us recall a basic point of Marian theology and Marian devotion. It is a time-honored thought of St. Ambrose that the recent Council recalled to us.[2] St. Ambrose describes Mary as *typus Ecclesiae*[3] or *figura Ecclesiae*.[4] And St. Augustine echoes this thought: *"Ipsa [Maria] figuram in se sanctae Ecclesiae."*[5] Why? Because her virginal procreation of Jesus is mystically reproduced in the Church's maternal and supernatural procreation of the faithful.

This parallel brings us even closer to Mary. Consider the fullness of grace that makes her *"tota pulchra,"*[6] blessed and immaculate. Do we not find some correspondence between that and the rich store of grace that was conferred on us when sacred ordination assimilated us to Christ through the charisms of holiness and ministerial grace? We would always do well to make Mary the mirror of our priesthood, our *speculum justitiae*.[7]

The line of thought goes on and on, moving from the mystical to the moral sphere. Mary is the model of the Church.[8] She "eminently embodies all the graces and perfections"[9] of the Church, which we are anxious and obliged to have. Mary is a teacher. She teaches us, whose duty it is to teach the People of God by doctrine and example. And what exactly does Mary teach us? The whole Gospel, as we well know.

VIRTUES FOR TODAY

But what specifically does she teach us today? Here our reflection turns into prayer: Mary, teach us to love. Mary obtains love. It was Mary who conceived Christ through the work of the Holy Spirit, the living embodiment of God's love. It was she who presided over the birth of the Church on the day of Pentecost, when the same Holy Spirit entered the group of disciples—the apostles first among them— and breathed a life of unity and charity into the mystical and historical body of Christians, into redeemed humanity. And we have come here to implore, through Mary's intercession, for the perduring continuation of this same miracle; to obtain from her, as from the source, a new flood of the Holy Spirit.

For we have rediscovered the ecclesial communion which, on the apostolic level, we call collegiality. It is an intercommunion of charity and apostolic effectiveness; and in this fateful era for the Church and the world, we wish to honor and implement it more effectively in thought and deed. We want to do this through love, through the love that gave Mary the power of procreating Christ. We earnestly ask for this love for ourselves, so that we may be capable of carrying out our mission to propagate Christ in the world. Above all, we ask for that love which descends to us as grace, and rises from us as a *fiat*, echoing Mary's. The *fiat* is our self-sacrifice and love, which we hope will burn unfailingly throughout our mortal life and become an immortal blaze.

PRIESTLY CELIBACY

Mary, we ask for love. We seek love for Christ: a love that is single-minded and total, a love that is self-giving, a love that is sacrificial. Mary, teach us to be what we already profess to know in humility and faith. Teach us to be immaculate as you are. Teach us to be chaste, that is, faithful to the sublime and awesome obligation of our sacred celibacy, which is so much discussed by many today, and misunderstood by some. We know well what celibacy is. It is more than a state, a continuing act, or a perpetually burning flame; it is a superhuman virtue, which therefore needs supernatural support.

Mary ever Virgin, make us understand now the paradoxical essence of this state, which is proper to the Latin priesthood and also to the episcopate and the religious state in the Eastern Churches. Likewise make us understand its value: its heroism, its beauty, its joy and its power. Teach us to understand the power and

honor of a ministry without reservations, a
ministry totally dedicated and devoted to the
service of human beings, to the crucifixion
of the flesh,[10] and to unconditional soldiering
for God's kingdom. Mary, help us to understand
anew this mysterious summons to follow Christ
totally and undividedly.[11] And teach us to love
accordingly.

Our prayer continues. We have noted that
the conciliar passages devoted to you, faithful
Virgin, acknowledge in you a primary virtue,
the primary virtue that unites us to God — faith.
If one makes a thoroughgoing diagnosis of the
needs confronting society and God's Church in
this turbulent hour, he will see that the Church
most needs one thing to be in communion with
Christ, with God and with man.

That one thing is faith, supernatural faith:
a faith that is simple, complete and strong;
a faith that is sincere and alive, imbibed at
its authentic source, the Word of God, and
its indefectible channel, the magisterium instituted and guaranteed by Christ.

You, Mary, are blessed because you believed.[12] Comfort us with your example, and
obtain this charism for us. How can we be
followers of Christ if doubt and denial destroy
our certainty?[13] How can we be witnesses,
like the apostles, if the truth of the faith grows
dim in our hearts?

We will also ask you, Mary, to give us
hope from your example and intercession.
Spes nostra, salve![14] For we also are greatly
in need of hope. Mary, as the Council said —

concluding its great document on the Church
— you are *Mater Ecclesiae*, Mother of the Church.
You are the image and the beginning of the
Church as it is to be perfected in the world
to come; and here on earth you shine out as
a sign of sure hope and comfort for the way-
faring People of God.[15]

—Homily at the concelebrated Mass as the Synod drew
toward its close, October 25, 1969 (TPS)

1. See St. Augustine: *PL* 40, 399.
2. Second Vatican Council, *Dogmatic Constitution on the Church*, no. 63 [*TPS* X, 398].
3. *PL* 15, 1555. Type of the Church.
4. *PL* 16, 326. Figure of the Church.
5. *PL* 40, 661. She embodied a figure of the holy Church herself.
6. Wholly beautiful.
7. Mirror of justice.
8. Second Vatican Council, *Dogmatic Constitution on the Church*, no. 53 [*TPS* X, 395].
9. Olier.
10. Gal. 5:24.
11. See Mt. 19:12.
12. Lk. 1:45.
13. See Jn. 6:67.
14. Hail [Mary], our hope!
15. Second Vatican Council, *Dogmatic Constitution on the Church*, no. 68 [*TPS* X, 399].

Mary, Our Hope

Our mind is still full of thoughts aroused by the feast of the Assumption of Mary into heaven which we celebrated yesterday. That feast reminds us, mortal citizens of the earth and pilgrims towards everlasting, perfect and blessed life of another kind, that that life has been promised and prepared for us too, as followers of that most pure and perfect woman who is the Mother of Christ.

Many thoughts arise as we look upon that blessed vision of Mary, from now on associated body and soul in the fullness of the divine happiness. One of the chief is that of the dignity of the human person, not only in its spiritual element, but also in its physical, corporeal element, which is part of it too. We ought to hold this enlightening idea firmly in our minds. Let us never forget two things: man is a composite being, made up of soul and body; this perfect complementary unity between soul and body, was disturbed in us by original sin. Sin miserably complicated man's moral functioning, and sullied the spiritual and physical beauty of our being. Hence we are for ever in search of this personal restoration which will give back to the soul dominion over the body and enable the body to let the soul shine through.

These reflections are a source of suffering and of hope. Of suffering, because we see prevailing today, in increasingly unprincipled demonstrations, the attempt to make the body the first priority of life, the unifying principle of the psychological and aesthetic harmony of life. It has reached the point, in recent days, of naturalistic and obscene displays, of the exaltation of nudism, exorcism, and "free love." Those who follow the newspapers know of the shameless displays to which we allude.

Animal man degrades himself without limit. Must we wonder, then, that pleasure, selfishness, delinquency and drugs are spreading like social epidemics which are debasing and saddening the quality of life.

But our reflection, deriving from the glorification of Mary, is also a source of hope: hope that the sense of dignity and purity will affirm itself in no less degree in our generation, especially among the ranks of the young, disdaining the hypocrisy which calls itself liberation from the "taboos" of decency and uprightness of behavior.

May they be aware that the Christian vocation requires the body to be subject to the soul, not without ascetic effort, and the soul to be united with God, with a certain anticipated experience of mystical blessedness and inward beauty.

Let us pray to the Madonna, dearly beloved, that she may strengthen in us this hope.

—*Angelus message, August 6, 1970 (OR)*

Mary Immaculate, Our Model

Today what interests us in the festive message of the Church? It is extraordinarily beautiful, but to understand and enjoy it, it is necessary to take account of the whole historical, moral and theological picture of humanity which present-day culture finds hard to garner and appreciate.

For us believers, the scene which has to be contemplated is immense and dramatic. It is constituted from the obscure depths of the fall of man and of all his progeny, among whom we are all included. It is the story of original sin because of which man as he now exists is no longer the true and perfect man whom God conceived and created: a being similar to Him, the splendid reflection of His countenance, all light and mystery.

We think too little of this general misfortune which altered and degraded the human figure and which is at the root of our troubles and the humbling and agitated experiences of our moral psychology. Right in the center of this universal scenario of misery there is raised up an exceptional and ideal figure, unsullied and unblemished, the object of

God's overwhelming love: the Lord is with you, Mary; you are the chosen one, the blessed among all women, excelling in goodness, beauty and immaculate purity, a woman unique and full of grace, the incomparable model of virgin and mother, chosen to offer stainless flesh to the Word of God, who in you, Mary, becomes our Brother, Teacher and Savior.

If we are Christians, if we seek the ways of our rehabilitation and final salvation, how can we ignore and disregard the Blessed Virgin, our sister, our mother, the lamp that leads to Christ?

It is stupendous, this view of Catholic truth, and of this we must always be convinced. It offers us a very human school of perfection. To whom is it offered? To all: to the afflicted, to the poor, to the humble and especially to the pure of heart. Let us say it again to the sons of our generation, assailed by so many profanations, tempted by so many allurements of permissive immorality, and who are perhaps already sceptical of the beauty and possibility of innocence as well as of the dignity of the body and the soul, and of the delicate relationship which distinguishes them and unites them.

Let us find in the Immaculate Conception the imperative summons, and let us find again the hope of the Christian way of life, the blessing promised to the pure of heart, that of recognizing the presence of God everywhere. May she help us in this regard.

—Angelus message, December 8, 1971 (OR)

Mary, the Symbol of Beauty and Purity

Today, beloved sons, is a great feast, not only because it is the August holiday, the traditional day for the summer vacation, but also because it is the feast of Mary, Mother of Christ, assumed into heaven. This truth, as you are aware, was defined as a dogma of faith in 1950 by our venerated predecessor, Pope Pius XII. The Assumption was a real event about which we should have no doubt; rather we should have for it in our faithful hearts certainty, joy, hope, seeking to understand the symbolic value which this miraculous fact holds in the economy of salvation and in Christian behavior.

The Assumption is the triumph not only of the most pure soul of her who was blessed among women, but likewise of her innocent, virginal and immaculate body. Just as the body of Jesus, her Son, was raised from the dead and thus invested with the divinity to which it was united in order to enjoy a higher form of life, so the body of Mary most pure, which by the power of the Holy Spirit, had generated the humanity of Christ, attains that fullness of perfection which is reserved to bodies after the blessed resurrection (cf. 1 Cor. 15:42ff.).

It is a programmatic lesson for us who, as children of our age, tend to materialize the human spirit and to subject it to the dominion of pleasure and the reign of the senses, by making of the flesh a temptation and a dark and illusory principle of corruption. On the other hand, our Lady assumed into heaven gives us the vision of the spiritualization of the flesh by making it resplendent in purity and beauty. It is, as it were, an invitation to us to give back again to the corporeal part of our being its dignity and its title, that is, true purity, in order to recover the superhuman immortality of the resurrection and of eternal life.

Worldly opinion might regard all of this as unreal, like the voice of a dream, or something out of fashion, so much does the decadence of public morality preach and profess the contrary. Let us therefore, if we are possessed of the Christian sense, seek to restore to the body its true nobility which the spirit quickens and reinvigorates and, if necessary, chastens in order to insure reaching the goal of the eternal and happy resurrection.

May our Lady assumed into heaven help us to relish physical purity and spiritual beauty.

—Angelus message, August 15, 1972 (OR)

The Rosary — Contemplation of the Mysteries of Salvation

The month of October is dedicated to the rosary, that popular devotion to Mary, Mother of Christ, in which we contemplate the cycle of salvation amid the rhythm of the "Ave Maria"; the rosary like so many roses forms a garland for the most beautiful, the more pure, the most holy of women, the blessed virgin and mother, who has a hundred unique titles: the new Eve, the Seat of Wisdom, the Immaculate, the Queen of Heaven, Mother of the Incarnate God, Mother of the Church...a litany without end.

The Marian calendar is not in contrast with the liturgical calendar, which is permeated by Christological doctrine and which celebrates the mystery of salvation; indeed, it breaks up and refracts its light to offer inexhaustible treasures to the humble prayers of the individual, of the Christian family, of the community.

To venerate the Madonna aids us in living our faith in "spirit and truth"; it helps us to follow the sublime and human example of Mary; and in doing so, we can ask her heavenly assistance in our daily needs as well as in the greater needs of the world today.

The plan of Providence, that is to say, the divine action in human affairs, avails itself of prayer for success; and so much the more if to our prayers there is added the more worthy intercession of Mary, the Mother of our Savior.

Let us look, dearly beloved people, at the world just now; and then beg the Madonna to obtain from the Lord the peace so greatly desired and in some countries perhaps now on its way. Let us pray for peace with the sweet and insistent rhythm of the rosary on our lips and in our hearts.

—Angelus message, October 1, 1972 (OR)

"The Pure Mirror of Holiness"

Let us together greet this day, the feast of Mary Immaculate, and let us greet it for all of us to whom it is offered. It is the day in which the Madonna, the Mother of Christ is recognized as being free from every fault, from every imperfection, even from the hereditary imperfection of original sin, and therefore should be admired and exalted in her primeval and complete beauty as God wished her to be, the pure mirror of holiness and goodness, the ideal and real type for mankind regenerated by Christ. An enchantment, but not a dream. A privilege, but not remote; rather it invites every Christian to experience its spell and savor its joy.

This very unusual but real vision becomes the symbol, example, light and comfort for us who are submerged in the modern world and who are dazzled by the blinding lights of the ostentatious seduction of the senses, bereft of true beauty, grace and innocence. We are surrounded by an environment polluted by licentious behavior and degrading and impudent vice.

Today restores to us the ideal concept of human life, of the dignity of our person and of civic and human morality, and it also gives us once more the confidence of being equal to our elevation to the plane of being children of God, brothers of Christ and inhabited within by the mystery of the Holy Spirit. To be pupils of Mary Immaculate, her children, her followers, her protected ones.

This practical and positive aspect of our devotion gives us courage to contribute towards defending in our days, the truth of love, the integrity of the family, the nobility of entertainment, the morality of community life, the ecology of our civilization which should neither be ashamed nor forgetful of being Christian. It has the Virgin Mother, Mary Immaculate, clothed in the sun, as the emblem of its hope and of its salvation.

And this is how we will salute her today in Piazza di Spagna.

—*Angelus message, December 8, 1972 (OR)*

With Mary
on Our Pilgrim Way
in Faith

You know about the Holy Year. It begins in the local churches on the forthcoming feast of Pentecost. It aims at being a period of spiritual and moral renewal, and at finding its character- istic expression in reconciliation, that is, in the recomposition of order, of which Christ is the principle, in the depths of the consciences of individual souls, the order of every man with God, the order of every human relationship in the harmony of community sentiments, in justice, concord, charity, peace.

PROPHETIC MOMENT

The Holy Year should be a kind of prophet- ic moment, Messianic awakening, Christian maturity of civilization, which sometimes had its ideal intuition in the poetry of the world, even secular poetry. What does the ancient and well-known prophecy of Virgil say, for example? You, young people, fresh from school, will remember it: "magnus ab integro saeculorum nascitur ordo" *(Buc.* IV); his was a lyrical inspiration; ours would like to be one of those conscious and collective efforts which produce, in the Church and in the world, a step upwards, a sign of Christian progress, a breakthrough on the plane of humanity imbued with the life-bringing Spirit of the kingdom of God.

Is ours a dream? An ideal, certainly, but it must not be an empty, unreal one. Difficult, certainly; and for us, men of little faith, a demand that is beyond our strength. To renew the spiritual and moral energies of the Church, and consequently, or concurrently those of our society, is a courageous aspiration, which makes tangible to us, if nothing else, the necessity of a superior, extrinsic assistance, but near to us, accessible to us, a compassionate, affectionate assistance, already marked out in a general plan of goodness and mercy. Such a plan that must needs exist, if it is true, as it is true, that mankind is called, freely but surely, to a destiny of salvation. What assistance? What can be the help that enables us to dare, to hope for the aims of the Holy Year? Who can obtain for us the marvelous result which, following the logical demands of the Council, we have proposed?

HUMBLE, GLORIOUS QUEEN

The Blessed Virgin, beloved sons, Holy Mary, the Mother of Christ the Savior, the Mother of the Church, our humble and glorious Queen.

Here there opens in front of us a great theological panorama, characteristic of Catholic doctrine, in which we see how the divine plan of salvation, offered to the world by the one Mediator between God and men, efficacious by His own power, Christ Jesus (cf. 1 Tm. 2:5; Heb. 12:24), is carried out with human cooperation, marvelously associated with the divine work (cf. H. De Lubac, *Méd. sur l'Egl.*, pp. 241ff.). And what human cooperation has been chosen in the history of our Christian destinies, first in function, dignity and efficiency, not purely instrumental and physical, but as a predestined, though free and perfectly docile factor, if not that of Mary? (cf. *Lumen Gentium,* 56)

Here there is no end to what could be said about the Blessed Virgin, for us, after firmly grasping the doctrine that places her at the center of the redeeming plan, first and, in a certain sense, indispensable beside Christ our Savior. It will be enough to recall and affirm how the renewing outcome of the Holy Year will depend on the superlative assistance of the Blessed Virgin. We need her help, her intercession. We must put on our program a particular cult for the Virgin Mary, if we wish the historico-spiritual event, for which we are preparing, to reach its real purposes.

NEED OF MARIAN CULT

Now we will merely condense in a twofold recommendation the advantage of this Marian cult, to which we entrust so many of our hopes. The first recommendation is a fundamental one:

we must know the Madonna better as the authentic and ideal model of redeemed humanity. Let us study this limpid creature, this Eve without sin, this daughter of God, in whose innocent, stupendous perfection, the creative, original, intact thought of God is mirrored. Mary is human beauty, not only aesthetic, but essential, ontological, in synthesis with divine Love, with goodness and humility, with the spirituality and the clear-sightedness of the "Magnificat." She is the Virgin, the Mother in the purest and most genuine sense; she is the Woman clothed with the sun (cf. Rv. 12:1), in beholding whom our eyes must be dazzled, so often offended and blinded as they are by the profaned and profaning images of the pagan and licentious environment by which we are surrounded and almost attacked.

Our Lady is the sublime "type" not only of the creature redeemed by Christ's merits, but also the "type" of humanity on its pilgrim way in faith. She is the figure of the Church, as St. Ambrose calls her (in Lc. II, 7; P.L. 15, 1555), and St. Augustine presents her to catechumens: "figuram in se sanctae Ecclesiae demonstrat" (De Symb. 1, P.L. 40, 661). If we have our eyes fixed on Mary, the blessed, we will be able to reconstitute in ourselves the line and the structure of the renewed Church.

PRAY TO MARY

And the second recommendation is no less important: we must have confidence in recourse to the intercession of the Blessed Virgin. We must pray to her, invoke her. She is admirable in herself, she is lovable to us. As in the Gospel (cf. Jn. 2:3ff.), she intervenes with her divine Son, and obtains from Him miracles that the ordinary course of events would not admit. She is kind, she is powerful. She knows human needs and sorrows. We must renew our devotion to the Blessed Virgin (cf. *Lumen Gentium*, 67), if we wish to obtain the Holy Spirit and be sincere followers of Christ Jesus. May her faith (cf. Lk. 1:45) lead us to the reality of the Gospel, and help us to celebrate properly the coming Holy Year.

With our apostolic blessing.

—General audience, May 30, 1973 (OR)

Mary — The One Full of Grace

On the morning of Saturday, December 8, the feast of the Immaculate Conception, the Holy Father addressed the following words to the faithful and tourists present in St. Peter's Square, before reciting the Angelus.

Happy feast day, beloved sons, happy feast of the Immaculate Conception! We like to think of it as a feast day for the whole human family and especially for us of the Christian family, of the Church, a very dear feast day because this celebration of Mary authorizes us, in fact obliges us to honor, always through the merits of Christ, a human creature in her pristine, native and complete perfection, a being such as God conceived and loved before original sin upset the ideal design, the image of God marvelously reflected in human nature. The image, indeed, has remained, but it is stained and distorted; baptism was necessary to restore our original dignity, but the tendency to disorder has remained; and we know, unfortunately, with what painful consequences.

In the Blessed Virgin, on the contrary, beauty is intact, elevated, rather, to a degree of the ideal and splendor, of which it is difficult for us even to form an adequate concept. Mary is the one full of grace, illuminated by the Holy Spirit. Perhaps she is the Woman clothed with the sun, of whom the Apocalypse speaks (12:1). She is truly a delight for the world, a divine masterpiece of the human race.

And she is ours. Humble, pious, sweet, poor, absolutely pure. She is the ideal daughter, the sister, friend, the merciful advocate of humanity.

So today, as is now our custom on this blessed day, we, too, will go to take flowers to the column that exalts her beautiful mystery in the heart of this Rome of ours. We would like our flowers to be your symbol too, Romans. The symbol of your piety, the symbol of your faith. We would like them to be a symbol of the common desire to preserve a Christian appearance for this prophetic City, a sense and a behavior of spiritual beauty. We would like them to be a symbol of the innocence of our children, the freshness and purity of our youth, the healthy and prosperous vitality of all our people, and of peace for the world.

Mary, the Immaculate, though unique in her innocence, as we were saying, is ours. Our exemplary type, our hope, because she is Mother of Christ and Mother of the Church. Let us honor her together, let us pray to her together.

—Angelus message, December 8, 1973 (OR)

Devotion to the Blessed Virgin Mary

(Marialis Cultus)

INTRODUCTION

Division of the Treatise, Occasion and Purpose of the Document

Venerable Brothers: Health and the Apostolic Blessing

From the moment when we were called to the See of Peter, we have constantly striven to enhance devotion to the Blessed Virgin Mary, not only with the intention of interpreting the sentiments of the Church and our own personal inclination but also because, as is well known, this devotion forms a very noble part of the whole sphere of that sacred worship in which there intermingle the highest expressions of wisdom and of religion[1] and which is therefore the primary task of the People of God.

Precisely with a view to this task, we have always favored and encouraged the great work of liturgical reform promoted by the Second Vatican Ecumenical Council; and it has certainly come about not without a particular design of divine Providence that the first conciliar document which together with the venerable Fathers we approved and signed *in Spiritu Sancto* was the Constitution *Sacro-sanctum concilium*. The purpose of this document was precisely to restore and enhance the liturgy and to make more fruitful the participation of the faithful in the sacred mysteries.[2] From that time onwards, many acts of our pontificate have been directed towards the improvement of divine worship, as is demonstrated by the fact that we have promulgated in these recent years numerous books of the Roman Rite, restored according to the principles and norms of the same Council. For this we profoundly thank the Lord, the giver of all good things, and we are grateful to the episcopal conferences and individual bishops who in various ways have collaborated with us in the preparation of these books.

We contemplate with joy and gratitude the work so far accomplished and the first positive results of the liturgical renewal, destined as they are to increase as this renewal comes to be understood in its basic purposes and correctly applied. At the same time we do not cease with vigilant solicitude to concern ourself with whatever can give orderly fulfillment to the renewal of the worship with which the Church in spirit and truth (cf. Jn. 4:24) adores the Father and the Son and the Holy Spirit, "venerates with special love Mary the most holy Mother of God"[3] and honors with religious devotion the memory of the martyrs and the other saints.

The development, desired by us, of devotion to the Blessed Virgin Mary is an indication of the Church's genuine piety. This devotion fits — as we have indicated above — into the only worship that is rightly called "Christian," because it takes its origin and effectiveness from Christ, finds its complete expression in Christ, and leads through Christ in the Spirit to the Father. In the sphere of worship this devotion necessarily reflects God's redemptive plan, in which a special form of veneration is appropriate to the singular place which Mary occupies in that plan.[4] Indeed every authentic development of Christian worship is necessarily followed by a fitting increase of veneration for the Mother of the Lord. Moreover, the history of piety shows how "the various forms of devotion towards the Mother of God that the Church has approved within the limits of wholesome and orthodox doctrine"[5] have developed in harmonious subordination to the worship of Christ, and have gravitated towards this worship as to their natural and necessary point of reference. The same is happening in our own time. The Church's reflection today on the mystery of Christ and on her own nature has led her to find at the root of the former and as a culmination of the latter the same figure of a woman: the Virgin Mary, the Mother of Christ and the Mother of the Church. And the increased knowledge of Mary's mission has become joyful veneration of her and adoring respect for the wise plan of God, who has

placed within His family (the Church), as in
every home, the figure of a Woman, who in a
hidden manner and in a spirit of service watches
over that family "and carefully looks after it
until the glorious day of the Lord."[6]

In our time, the changes that have occurred in social behavior, people's sensibilities, manners of expression in art and letters
and in the forms of social communication
have also influenced the manifestations of
religious sentiment. Certain practices of piety
that not long ago seemed suitable for expressing the religious sentiment of individuals
and of Christian communities seem today
inadequate or unsuitable because they are
linked with social and cultural patterns of
the past. On the other hand, in many places
people are seeking new ways of expressing
the unchangeable relationship of creatures
with their Creator, of children with their Father. In some people this may cause tem-
porary confusion. But anyone who with trust
in God reflects upon these phenomena dis-
covers that many tendencies of modern piety
(for example, the interiorization of religious
sentiment) are meant to play their part in the
development of Christian piety in general
and devotion to the Blessed Virgin in particular. Thus our own time, faithfully attentive
to tradition and to the progress of theology
and the sciences, will make its contribution
of praise to her whom, according to her own
prophetical words, all generations will call
blessed (cf. Lk. 1:48).

We therefore judge it in keeping with our apostolic service, venerable Brothers, to deal, in a sort of dialogue, with a number of themes connected with the place that the Blessed Virgin occupies in the Church's worship. These themes have already been partly touched upon by the Second Vatican Council[7] and also by ourself,[8] but it is useful to return to them in order to remove doubts and, especially, to help the development of that devotion to the Blessed Virgin which in the Church is motivated by the Word of God and practiced in the Spirit of Christ.

We therefore wish to dwell upon a number of questions concerning the relationship between the sacred liturgy and devotion to the Blessed Virgin (I), to offer considerations and directives suitable for favoring the development of that devotion (II) and finally to put forward a number of reflections intended to encourage the restoration, in a dynamic and more informed manner, of the recitation of the rosary, the practice of which was so strongly recommended by our predecessors and is so widely diffused among the Christian people (III).

PART ONE

Devotion to the Blessed Virgin Mary in the Liturgy

1. As we prepare to discuss the place which the Blessed Virgin Mary occupies in Christian worship, we must first turn our attention to the sacred liturgy. In addition to its rich doctrinal content, the liturgy has an incomparable pastoral effectiveness and a recognized exemplary value for the other forms of worship. We would have liked to take into consideration the various liturgies of the East and the West, but for the purpose of this document we shall dwell almost exclusively on the books of the Roman Rite. In fact, in accordance with the practical norms issued by the Second Vatican Council,[9] it is this Rite alone which has been the object of profound renewal. This is true also in regard to expressions of veneration for Mary. This Rite therefore deserves to be carefully considered and evaluated.

Section One
THE BLESSED VIRGIN IN THE REVISED ROMAN LITURGY

2. The reform of the Roman liturgy presupposed a careful restoration of its *General Calendar.* This Calendar is arranged in such a way as to give fitting prominence to the celebration on appropriate days of the work of salvation. It distributes throughout the year the whole mystery of Christ, from the Incarnation to the expectation of His return in glory,[10] and thus makes it possible in a more organic and closely-knit fashion to include the commemoration of Christ's Mother in the annual cycle of the mysteries of her Son.

3. For example, during Advent there are many liturgical references to Mary besides the Solemnity of December 8, which is a joint celebration of the Immaculate Conception of Mary, of the basic preparation (cf. Is. 11:1, 10) for the coming of the Savior and of the happy beginning of the Church without spot or wrinkle.[11] Such liturgical references are found especially on the days from December 17 to 24, and more particularly on the Sunday before Christmas, which recalls the ancient prophecies concerning the Virgin Mother and the Messiah[12] and includes readings from the Gospel concerning the imminent birth of Christ and His precursor.[13]

4. In this way the faithful, living in the liturgy the spirit of Advent, by thinking about the inexpressible love with which the Virgin

Mother awaited her Son,[14] are invited to take her as a model and to prepare themselves to meet the Savior who is to come. They must be "vigilant in prayer and joyful in...praise." [15] We would also remark that the Advent liturgy, by linking the awaiting of the Messiah and the awaiting of the glorious return of Christ with the admirable commemoration of His Mother, presents a happy balance in worship. This balance can be taken as a norm for preventing any tendency (as has happened at times in certain forms of popular piety) to separate devotion to the Blessed Virgin from its necessary point of reference — Christ. It also ensures that this season, as liturgy experts have noted, should be considered as a time particularly suited to devotion to the Mother of the Lord. This is an orientation that we confirm and which we hope to see accepted and followed everywhere.

5. The Christmas season is a prolonged commemoration of the divine, virginal and salvific motherhood of her whose "inviolate virginity brought the Savior into the world." [16] In fact, on the Solemnity of the Birth of Christ the Church both adores the Savior and venerates His glorious Mother. On the Epiphany, when she celebrates the universal call to salvation, the Church contemplates the Blessed Virgin, the true Seat of Wisdom and true Mother of the King, who presents to the wise men, for their adoration, the Redeemer of all peoples (cf. Mt. 2:11). On the Feast of the Holy

Family of Jesus, Mary and Joseph (the Sunday within the octave of Christmas) the Church meditates with profound reverence upon the holy life led in the house of Nazareth by Jesus, the Son of God and Son of Man, Mary His Mother, and Joseph the just man (cf. Mt. 1:19).

In the revised ordering of the Christmas period it seems to us that the attention of all should be directed towards the restored Solemnity of Mary the holy Mother of God. This celebration, placed on January 1 in conformity with the ancient indication of the liturgy of the City of Rome, is meant to commemorate the part played by Mary in this mystery of salvation. It is meant also to exalt the singular dignity which this mystery brings to the "holy Mother...through whom we were found worthy to receive the Author of life." [17] It is likewise a fitting occasion for renewing adoration of the newborn Prince of Peace, for listening once more to the glad tidings of the angels (cf. Lk. 2:14), and for imploring from God, through the Queen of Peace, the supreme gift of peace. It is for this reason that, in the happy concurrence of the octave of Christmas and the first day of the year, we have instituted the World Day of Peace, an occasion that is gaining increasing support and already bringing forth fruits of peace in the hearts of many.

6. To the two solemnities already mentioned (the Immaculate Conception and the Divine Motherhood) should be added the ancient and venerable celebrations of March 25 and August 15.

For the solemnity of the Incarnation of the Word, in the Roman Calendar the ancient title — the Annunciation of the Lord — has been deliberately restored, but the feast was and is a joint one of Christ and of the Blessed Virgin: of the Word, who becomes "Son of Mary" (Mk. 6:3), and of the Virgin, who becomes Mother of God. With regard to Christ, the East and the West, in the inexhaustible riches of their liturgies, celebrate this solemnity as the commemoration of the salvific "fiat" of the Incarnate Word, who, entering the world, said: "God, here I am! I am coming to obey Your will" (cf. Heb. 10:7; Ps. 39:8-9). They commemorate it as the beginning of the redemption and of the indissoluble and wedded union of the divine nature with human nature in the one Person of the Word. With regard to Mary, these liturgies celebrate it as a feast of the new Eve, the obedient and faithful virgin, who with her generous "fiat" (cf. Lk. 1:38) became through the working of the Spirit the Mother of God, but also the true Mother of the living, and, by receiving into her womb the one Mediator (cf. 1 Tm. 2:5), became the true Ark of the Covenant and true Temple of God. These liturgies celebrate it as a culminating moment in the salvific dialogue between God and man, and as a commemoration of the Blessed Virgin's free consent and cooperation in the plan of redemption.

The solemnity of August 15 celebrates the glorious Assumption of Mary into heaven.

It is a feast of her destiny of fullness and blessedness, of the glorification of her immaculate soul and of her virginal body, of her perfect configuration to the Risen Christ; a feast that sets before the eyes of the Church and of all mankind the image and the consoling proof of the fulfillment of their final hope, namely, that this full glorification is the destiny of all those whom Christ has made His brothers, having "flesh and blood in common with them" (Heb. 2:14; cf. Gal. 4:4). The solemnity of the Assumption is prolonged in the celebration of the Queenship of the Blessed Virgin Mary, which occurs seven days later. On this occasion we contemplate her who, seated beside the King of ages, shines forth as Queen and intercedes as Mother.[18] These four solemnities, therefore, mark with the highest liturgical rank the main dogmatic truths concerning the handmaid of the Lord.

7. After the solemnities just mentioned, particular consideration must be given to those celebrations that commemorate salvific events in which the Blessed Virgin was closely associated with her Son. Such are the feasts of the Nativity of our Lady (September 8), "the hope of the entire world and the dawn of salvation"[19]; and the Visitation (May 31), in which the liturgy recalls the "Blessed Virgin Mary carrying her Son within her,"[20] and visiting Elizabeth to offer charitable assistance and to proclaim the mercy of God the Savior.[21] Then there is the commemoration of Our Lady of Sorrows (September 15), a fitting

occasion for reliving a decisive moment in the history of salvation and for venerating, together with the Son "lifted up on the cross, His suffering Mother." [22]

The feast of February 2, which has been given back its ancient name, the Presentation of the Lord, should also be considered as a joint commemoration of the Son and of the Mother, if we are fully to appreciate its rich content. It is the celebration of a mystery of salvation accomplished by Christ, a mystery with which the Blessed Virgin was intimately associated as the Mother of the Suffering Servant of Yahweh, as the one who performs a mission belonging to ancient Israel, and as the model for the new People of God, which is ever being tested in its faith and hope by suffering and persecution (cf. Lk. 2:21-35).

8. The restored Roman Calendar gives particular prominence to the celebrations listed above, but it also includes other kinds of commemorations connected with local devotions and which have acquired a wider popularity and interest (e.g., February 11, Our Lady of Lourdes; August 5, the Dedication of the Basilica of St. Mary Major). Then there are others, originally celebrated by particular religious families but which today, by reason of the popularity they have gained, can truly be considered ecclesial (e.g., July 16, Our Lady of Mount Carmel; October 7, Our Lady of the Rosary). There are still others which, apart from their apocryphal content, present lofty and exemplary values and carry on venerable

traditions having their origin especially in the
East (e.g., the Immaculate Heart of the Blessed
Virgin, celebrated on the Saturday following
the second Sunday after Pentecost).

9. Nor must one forget that the General
Roman Calendar does not include all celebrations in honor of the Blessed Virgin. Rather,
it is for individual Calendars to include, with
fidelity to liturgical norms but with sincere en-
dorsement, the Marian feasts proper to the
different local churches. Lastly, it should be
noted that frequent commemorations of the
Blessed Virgin are possible through the use of
the Saturday Masses of our Lady. This is an
ancient and simple commemoration and one
that is made very adaptable and varied by the
flexibility of the modern Calendar and the
number of formulas provided by the Missal.

10. In this Apostolic Exhortation we do not
intend to examine the whole content of the new
Roman Missal. But by reason of the work of
evaluation that we have undertaken to carry
out in regard to the revised books of the Roman
Rite,[23] we would like to mention some of the aspects and themes of the Missal. In the first place,
we are pleased to note how the Eucharistic
Prayers of the Missal, in admirable harmony
with the Eastern liturgies,[24] contain a significant
commemoration of the Blessed Virgin. For
example, the ancient Roman Canon, which
commemorates the Mother of the Lord in terms
full of doctrine and devotional inspiration:
"In union with the whole Church we honor
Mary, the ever-virgin Mother of Jesus Christ

our Lord and God." In a similar way the recent Eucharistic Prayer III expresses with intense supplication the desire of those praying to share with the Mother the inheritance of sons: "May he make us an everlasting gift to you [the Father] and enable us to share in the inheritance of your saints, with Mary, the Virgin Mother of God." This daily commemoration, by reason of its place at the heart of the divine Sacrifice, should be considered a particularly expressive form of the veneration that the Church pays to the "Blessed of the Most High" (cf. Lk. 1:28).

11. As we examine the texts of the revised Missal we see how the great Marian themes of the Roman prayerbook have been accepted in perfect doctrinal continuity with the past. Thus, for example, we have the themes of Mary's Immaculate Conception and fullness of grace, the divine motherhood, the unblemished and fruitful virginity, the Temple of the Holy Spirit, Mary's cooperation in the work of her Son, her exemplary sanctity, merciful intercession, assumption into heaven, maternal Queenship and many other themes. We also see how other themes, in a certain sense new ones, have been introduced in equally perfect harmony with the theological developments of the present day. Thus, for example, we have the theme of Mary and the Church, which has been inserted into the texts of the Missal in a variety of aspects, a variety that matches the many and varied relations that exist between the Mother of Christ and the Church. For example, in the celebration of the Immaculate

Conception which texts recognize the beginning of the Church, the spotless Bride of Christ.[25] In the assumption they recognize the beginning that has already been made and the image of what, for the whole Church, must still come to pass.[26] In the mystery of Mary's motherhood they confess that she is the Mother of the Head and of the members—the holy Mother of God and therefore the provident Mother of the Church.[27]

When the liturgy turns its gaze either to the primitive Church or to the Church of our own days it always finds Mary. In the primitive Church she is seen praying with the apostles[28]; in our own day she is actively present, and the Church desires to live the mystery of Christ with her: "Grant that your Church which with Mary shared Christ's passion may be worthy to share also in his resurrection."[29] She is also seen represented as a voice of praise in unison with which the Church wishes to give glory to God: "...with her [Mary] may we always praise you."[30] And since the liturgy is worship that requires a way of living consistent with it, it asks that devotion to the Blessed Virgin should become a concrete and deeply-felt love for the Church, as is wonderfully expressed in the prayer after the Communion in the Mass of September 15: "...that as we recall the sufferings shared by the Blessed Virgin Mary, we may with the Church fulfill in ourselves what is lacking in the sufferings of Christ."

12. The Lectionary is one of the books of the Roman Rite that has greatly benefited from

the post-conciliar reform, by reason both of its added texts and of the intrinsic value of these texts, which contain the ever-living and efficacious word of God (cf. Heb. 4:12). This rich collection of biblical texts has made it possible to arrange the whole history of salvation in an orderly three-year cycle and to set forth more completely the mystery of Christ. The logical consequence has been that the Lectionary contains a larger number of Old and New Testament readings concerning the Blessed Virgin. This numerical increase has not however been based on random choice: only those readings have been accepted which in different ways and degrees can be considered Marian, either from the evidence of their content or from the results of careful exegesis, supported by the teachings of the magisterium or by solid Tradition. It is also right to observe that these readings occur not only on feasts of the Blessed Virgin but are read on many other occasions, for example on certain Sundays during the liturgical year,[31] in the celebration of rites that deeply concern the Christian's sacramental life and the choices confronting him,[32] as also in the joyful or sad experiences of his life on earth.[33]

13. The Liturgy of the Hours, the revised book of the Office, also contains outstanding examples of devotion to the Mother of the Lord. These are to be found in the hymns—which include several masterpieces of universal literature, such as Dante's sublime prayer to the Blessed Virgin[34]—and in the antiphons that complete the daily Office. To these lyrical

invocations there has been added the well-known prayer *Sub tuum praesidium*, venerable for its antiquity and admirable for its content. Other examples occur in the prayers of intercession at Lauds and Vespers, prayers which frequently express trusting recourse to the Mother of mercy. Finally there are selections from the vast treasury of writings on our Lady composed by authors of the first Christian centuries, of the Middle Ages and of modern times.

14. The commemoration of the Blessed Virgin occurs often in the Missal, the Lectionary and the Liturgy of the Hours—the hinges of the liturgical prayer of the Roman Rite. In the other revised liturgical books also expressions of love and suppliant veneration addressed to the Theotokos are not lacking. Thus the Church invokes her, the Mother of grace, before immersing candidates in the saving waters of Baptism[35]; the Church invokes her intercession for mothers who, full of gratitude for the gift of motherhood, come to church to express their joy[36]; the Church holds her up as a model to those who follow Christ by embracing the religious life[37] or who receive the Consecration of Virgins.[38] For these people the Church asks Mary's motherly assistance.[39] The Church prays fervently to Mary on behalf of her children who have come to the hour of their death.[40] The Church asks Mary's intercession for those who have closed their eyes to the light of this world and appeared before Christ, the eternal Light[41]; and the Church, through Mary's prayers, invokes

comfort upon those who in sorrow mourn with faith the departure of their loved ones.[42]

15. The examination of the revised liturgical books leads us to the comforting observation that the postconciliar renewal has, as was previously desired by the liturgical movement, properly considered the Blessed Virgin in the mystery of Christ, and, in harmony with tradition, has recognized the singular place that belongs to her in Christian worship as the holy Mother of God and the worthy Associate of the Redeemer.

It could not have been otherwise. If one studies the history of Christian worship, in fact, one notes that both in the East and in the West the highest and purest expressions of devotion to the Blessed Virgin have sprung from the liturgy or have been incorporated into it.

We wish to emphasize the fact that the veneration which the universal Church today accords to blessed Mary is a derivation from and an extension and unceasing increase of the devotion that the Church of every age has paid to her, with careful attention to truth and with an ever watchful nobility of expression. From perennial Tradition kept alive by reason of the uninterrupted presence of the Spirit and continual attention to the Word, the Church of our time draws motives, arguments and incentives for the veneration that she pays to the Blessed Virgin. And the liturgy, which receives approval and strength from the magisterium, is a most lofty expression and an evident proof of this living Tradition.

Section One

THE BLESSED VIRGIN AS THE MODEL OF THE CHURCH IN DIVINE WORSHIP

16. In accordance with some of the guidelines of the Council's teaching on Mary and the Church, we now wish to examine more closely a particular aspect of the relationship between Mary and the liturgy — namely, Mary as a model of the spiritual attitude with which the Church celebrates and lives the divine mysteries. That the Blessed Virgin is an exemplar in this field derives from the fact that she is recognized as a most excellent exemplar of the Church in the order of faith, charity and perfect union with Christ,[43] that is, of that interior disposition with which the Church, the beloved spouse, closely associated with her Lord, invokes Christ and through Him worships the eternal Father.[44]

17. Mary is *the attentive Virgin*, who receives the word of God with faith, that faith which in her case was the gateway and path to divine motherhood, for, as St. Augustine realized, "Blessed Mary by believing conceived Him [Jesus] whom believing she brought forth."[45] In fact, when she received from the angel the answer to her doubt (cf. Lk. 1:34-37), "full of faith, and conceiving Christ in her mind before conceiving Him in her womb, she

said, 'I am the handmaid of the Lord, let what you have said be done to me' (Lk. 1:38)."[46] It was faith that was for her the cause of blessedness and certainty in the fulfillment of the promise: "Blessed is she who believed that the promise made her by the Lord would be fulfilled" (Lk. 1:45). Similarly, it was faith with which she, who played a part in the Incarnation and was a unique witness to it, thinking back on the events of the infancy of Christ, meditated upon these events in her heart (cf. Lk. 2:19, 51). The Church also acts in this way, especially in the liturgy, when with faith she listens, accepts, proclaims and venerates the word of God, distributes it to the faithful as the bread of life[47] and in the light of that word examines the signs of the times and interprets and lives the events of history.

18. Mary is also *the Virgin in prayer.* She appears as such in the visit to the mother of the precursor, when she pours out her soul in expressions glorifying God, and expressions of humility, faith and hope. This prayer is the Magnificat (cf. Lk. 1:46-55), Mary's prayer par excellence, the song of the messianic times in which there mingles the joy of the ancient and the new Israel. As St. Irenaeus seems to suggest, it is in Mary's canticle that there was heard once more the rejoicing of Abraham who foresaw the Messiah (cf. Jn. 8:56)[48] and there rang out in prophetic anticipation the voice of the Church: "In her exultation Mary prophetically declared in the name of the Church: 'My soul proclaims the glory of the Lord....'"[49] And in fact Mary's

hymn has spread far and wide and has become the prayer of the whole Church in all ages.

At Cana, Mary appears once more as the Virgin in prayer: when she tactfully told her Son of a temporal need, she also obtained an effect of grace, namely, that Jesus, in working the first of His "signs," confirmed His disciples' faith in Him (cf. Jn. 2:1-12).

Likewise, the last description of Mary's life presents her as praying. The apostles "joined in continuous prayer, together with several women, including Mary the mother of Jesus, and with his brothers" (Acts 1:14). We have here the prayerful presence of Mary in the early Church and in the Church throughout all ages, for, having been assumed into heaven, she has not abandoned her mission of intercession and salvation.[50] The title Virgin in prayer also fits the Church, which day by day presents to the Father the needs of her children, "praises the Lord unceasingly and intercedes for the salvation of the world."[51]

19. Mary is also *the Virgin-Mother* — she who "believing and obeying...brought forth on earth the Father's Son. This she did, not knowing man but overshadowed by the Holy Spirit."[52] This was a miraculous motherhood, set up by God as the type and exemplar of the fruitfulness of the Virgin-Church, which "becomes herself a mother.... For by her preaching and by baptism she brings forth to a new and immortal life children who are conceived by the power of the Holy Spirit and born of God."[53] The ancient Fathers rightly taught that the

Church prolongs in the sacrament of Baptism the virginal motherhood of Mary. Among such references we like to recall that of our illustrious predecessor, St. Leo the Great, who in a Christmas homily says: "The origin which [Christ] took in the womb of the Virgin He has given to the baptismal font: He has given to water what He had given to His Mother—the power of the Most High and the overshadowing of the Holy Spirit (cf. Lk. 1:35), which was responsible for Mary's bringing forth the Savior, has the same effect, so that water may regenerate the believer." [54] If we wished to go to liturgical sources, we could quote the beautiful *Illatio* of the Mozarabic liturgy: "The former [Mary] carried Life in her womb; the latter [the Church] bears Life in the waters of baptism. In Mary's members Christ was formed; in the waters of the Church Christ is put on." [55]

20. Mary is, finally, *the Virgin presenting offerings*. In the episode of the Presentation of Jesus in the Temple (cf. Lk. 2:22-35), the Church, guided by the Spirit, has detected, over and above the fulfillment of the laws regarding the offering of the firstborn (cf. Ex. 13:11-16) and the purification of the mother (cf. Lv. 12:6-8), a mystery of salvation related to the history of salvation. That is, she has noted the continuity of the fundamental offering that the Incarnate Word made to the Father when He entered the world (cf. Heb. 15:5-7). The Church has seen the universal nature of salvation proclaimed, for Simeon, greeting in the Child the light to enlighten the peoples and the glory of the people

Israel (cf. Lk. 2:32), recognized in Him the Messiah, the Savior of all. The Church has understood the prophetic reference to the passion of Christ: the fact that Simeon's words, which linked in one prophecy the Son as "the sign of contradiction" (Lk. 2:34) and the Mother, whose soul would be pierced by a sword (cf. Lk. 2:35), came true on Calvary. A mystery of salvation, therefore, that in its various aspects orients the episode of the Presentation in the Temple to the salvific event of the cross. But the Church herself, in particular from the Middle Ages onwards, has detected in the heart of the Virgin taking her Son to Jerusalem to present Him to the Lord (cf. Lk. 2:22) a desire to make an offering, a desire that exceeds the ordinary meaning of the rite. A witness to this intuition is found in the loving prayer of St. Bernard: "Offer your Son, holy Virgin, and present to the Lord the blessed fruit of your womb. Offer for the reconciliation of us all the holy Victim which is pleasing to God." [56]

This union of the Mother and the Son in the work of redemption[57] reaches its climax on Calvary, where Christ "offered himself as the perfect sacrifice to God" (Heb. 9:14) and where Mary stood by the cross (cf. Jn. 19:25), "suffering grievously with her only-begotten Son. There she united herself with a maternal heart to His sacrifice, and lovingly consented to the immolation of this victim which she herself had brought forth" [58] and also was offering to the eternal Father.[59] To perpetuate down the centuries the sacrifice of the cross, the divine Savior instituted the Eucharistic Sacrifice, the memorial of His death and resurrection, and entrusted it to His spouse the Church,[60] which, especially on Sundays, calls the faithful together to celebrate the Passover of the Lord until He comes again.[61] This the Church does in union with the saints in heaven and in particular with the Blessed Virgin,[62] whose burning charity and unshakeable faith she imitates.

21. Mary is not only an example for the whole Church in the exercise of divine worship but is also, clearly, a teacher of the spiritual life for individual Christians. The faithful at a very early date began to look to Mary and to imitate her in making their lives an act of worship of God and making their worship a commitment of their lives. As early as the fourth century, St. Ambrose, speaking to the people, expressed the hope that each of them would have the spirit of Mary in order to glorify God: "May the heart of Mary be in each Christian to proclaim the greatness of the Lord; may her spirit be in everyone to exult in God."[63] But Mary is above all the example of that worship that consists in making one's life an offering to God. This is an ancient and ever new doctrine that each individual can hear again by heeding the Church's teaching, but also by heeding the very voice of the Virgin as she, anticipating in herself the wonderful petition of the Lord's prayer—"Your will be done" (Mt. 6:10)—replied to God's messenger: "I am the handmaid of the Lord. Let what you have said be done to me" (Lk. 1:38). And Mary's "yes" is for all

Christians a lesson and example of obedience to the will of the Father, which is the way and means of one's own sanctification.

22. It is also important to note how the Church expresses in various effective attitudes of devotion the many relationships that bind her to Mary: in profound veneration, when she reflects on the singular dignity of the Virgin who, through the action of the Holy Spirit, has become Mother of the Incarnate Word; in burning love, when she considers the spiritual motherhood of Mary towards all members of the Mystical Body; in trusting invocation, when she experiences the intercession of her advocate and helper[64]; in loving service, when she sees in the humble handmaid of the Lord the Queen of mercy and the Mother of grace; in zealous imitation, when she contemplates the holiness and virtues of her who is "full of grace" (Lk. 1:28); in profound wonder, when she sees in her, "as in a faultless model, that which she herself wholly desires and hopes to be"[65]; in attentive study, when she recognizes in the associate of the Redeemer, who already shares fully in the fruits of the Paschal Mystery, the prophetic fulfillment of her own future, until the day on which, when she has been purified of every spot and wrinkle (cf. Eph. 5:27), she will become like a bride arrayed for the bridegroom, Jesus Christ (cf. Rv. 21:2).

23. Therefore, venerable brothers, as we consider the piety that the liturgical Tradition of the universal Church and the renewed Roman Rite expresses towards the holy Mother of God,

and as we remember that the liturgy through its pre-eminent value as worship constitutes the golden norm for Christian piety, and finally as we observe how the Church when she celebrates the sacred mysteries assumes an attitude of faith and love similar to that of the Virgin, we realize the rightness of the exhortation that the Second Vatican Council addresses to all the children of the Church, namely "that the cult, especially the liturgical cult, of the Blessed Virgin be generously fostered." [66] This is an exhortation that we would like to see accepted everywhere without reservation and put into zealous practice.

PART TWO

The Renewal of
Devotion to Mary

24. The Second Vatican Council also exhorts us to promote other forms of piety side by side with liturgical worship, especially those recommended by the magisterium.[67] However, as is well known, the piety of the faithful and their veneration of the Mother of God has taken on many forms according to circumstances of time and place, the different sensibilities of peoples and their different cultural traditions. Hence it is that the forms in which this devotion is expressed, being subject to the ravages of time, show the need for a renewal that will permit them to substitute elements that are transient, to emphasize the elements that are ever new and to incorporate the doctrinal data obtained from theological reflection and the proposals of the Church's magisterium. This shows the need for episcopal conferences, local churches, religious families and communities of the faithful to promote a genuine

creative activity and at the same time to pro-
ceed to a careful revision of expressions and
exercises of piety directed towards the Blessed
Virgin. We would like this revision to be respect-
ful of wholesome tradition and open to the
legitimate requests of the people of our time.
It seems fitting, therefore, venerable brothers,
to put forward some principles for action in
this field.

Section One

TRINITARIAN, CHRISTOLOGICAL AND ECCLESIAL ASPECTS OF DEVOTION TO THE BLESSED VIRGIN

25. In the first place it is supremely fitting
that exercises of piety directed towards the
Virgin Mary should clearly express the Trinitarian and Christological note that is intrinsic
and essential to them. Christian worship in
fact is of itself worship offered to the Father
and to the Son and to the Holy Spirit, or, as the
liturgy puts it, to the Father through Christ
in the Spirit. From this point of view worship
is rightly extended, though in a substantially
different way, first and foremost and in a special
manner, to the Mother of the Lord and then to
the saints, in whom the Church proclaims the
Paschal Mystery, for they have suffered with
Christ and have been glorified with Him.[68]
In the Virgin Mary everything is relative to
Christ and dependent upon Him. It was with
a view to Christ that God the Father from all
eternity chose her to be the all-holy Mother
and adorned her with gifts of the Spirit granted

to no one else. Certainly genuine Christian
piety has never failed to highlight the indissoluble link and essential relationship of the
Virgin to the divine Savior.[69] Yet it seems to
us particularly in conformity with the spiritual
orientation of our time, which is dominated and
absorbed by the "question of Christ,"[70] that in
the expressions of devotion to the Virgin the
Christological aspect should have particular
prominence. It likewise seems to us fitting that
these expressions of devotion should reflect
God's plan, which laid down "with one single
degree the origin of Mary and the Incarnation
of the divine Wisdom."[71] This will without
doubt contribute to making piety towards the
Mother of Jesus more solid, and to making it
an effective instrument for attaining to full
"knowledge of the Son of God, until we become
the perfect man, fully mature with the fullness
of Christ himself" (Eph. 4:13). It will also
contribute to increasing the worship due to
Christ Himself, since, according to the perennial mind of the Church authoritatively repeated
in our own day,[72] "what is given to the handmaid is referred to the Lord; thus what is given
to the Mother redounds to the Son;...and
thus what is given as humble tribute to the
Queen becomes honor rendered to the King."[73]

26. It seems to us useful to add to this mention of the Christological orientation of devotion
to the Blessed Virgin a reminder of the fitting-
ness of giving prominence in this devotion
to one of the essential facts of the Faith: the
Person and work of the Holy Spirit. Theological

reflection and the liturgy have in fact noted how the sanctifying intervention of the Spirit in the Virgin of Nazareth was a culminating moment of the Spirit's action in the history of salvation. Thus, for example, some Fathers and writers of the Church attributed to the work of the Spirit the original holiness of Mary, who was as it were "fashioned by the Holy Spirit into a kind of new substance and new creature." [74] Reflecting on the Gospel texts — "The Holy Spirit will come upon you and the power of the Most High will cover you with his shadow" (Lk. 1:35) and "[Mary] was found to be with child through the Holy Spirit.... She has conceived what is in her by the Holy Spirit" (Mt. 1:18, 20) — they saw in the Spirit's intervention an action that consecrated and made fruitful Mary's virginity [75] and transformed her into the "Abode of the King" or "Bridal Chamber of the Word," [76] the "Temple" or "Tabernacle of the Lord," [77] the "Ark of the Covenant" or "the Ark of Holiness," [78] titles rich in biblical echoes. Examining more deeply still the mystery of the Incarnation, they saw in the mysterious relationship between the Spirit and Mary an aspect redolent of marriage, poetically portrayed by Prudentius: "The unwed Virgin espoused the Spirit," [79] and they called her the "Temple of the Holy Spirit," [80] an expression that emphasizes the sacred character of the Virgin, now the permanent dwelling of the Spirit of God. Delving deeply into the doctrine of the Paraclete, they saw that from Him as from a spring there flowed forth the fullness of grace (cf. Lk. 1:28) and the abundance of gifts that adorned her. Thus they attributed to the Spirit the faith, hope and charity that animated the Virgin's heart, the strength that sustained her acceptance of the will of God, and the vigor that upheld her in her suffering at the foot of the cross.[81] In Mary's prophetic canticle (cf. Lk. 1:46-55) they saw a special working of the Spirit who had spoken through the mouths of the prophets.[82] Considering, finally, the presence of the Mother of Jesus in the Upper Room, where the Spirit came down upon the infant Church (cf. Acts 1:12-14; 2:1-4), they enriched with new developments the ancient theme of Mary and the Church.[83] Above all they had recourse to the Virgin's intercession in order to obtain from the Spirit the capacity for engendering Christ in their own soul, as is attested to by St. Ildephonsus in a prayer of supplication, amazing in its doctrine and prayerful power: "I beg you, holy Virgin, that I may have Jesus from the Holy Spirit, by whom you brought Jesus forth. May my soul receive Jesus through the Holy Spirit by whom your flesh conceived Jesus.... May I love Jesus in the Holy Spirit in whom you adore Jesus as Lord and gaze upon Him as your Son."[84]

27. It is sometimes said that many spiritual writings today do not sufficiently reflect the whole doctrine concerning the Holy Spirit. It is the task of specialists to verify and weigh the truth of this assertion, but it is our task to exhort everyone, especially those in the pastoral ministry and also theologians, to meditate more

deeply on the working of the Holy Spirit in the history of salvation, and to ensure that Christian spiritual writings give due prominence to His life-giving action. Such a study will bring out in particular the hidden relationship between the Spirit of God and the Virgin of Nazareth, and show the influence they exert on the Church. From a more profound meditation on the truths of the Faith will flow a more vital piety.

28. It is also necessary that exercises of piety with which the faithful honor the Mother of the Lord should clearly show the place she occupies in the Church: "the highest place and the closest to us after Christ." [85] The liturgical buildings of Byzantine rite, both in the architectural structure itself and in the use of images, show clearly Mary's place in the Church. On the central door of the iconostasis there is a representation of the annunciation and in the apse an image of the glorious Theotokos. In this way one perceives how through the assent of the humble handmaid of the Lord mankind begins its return to God and sees in the glory of the all-holy Virgin the goal towards which it is journeying. The symbolism by which a church building demonstrates Mary's place in the mystery of the Church is full of significance and gives grounds for hoping that the different forms of devotion to the Blessed Virgin may everywhere be open to ecclesial perspectives.

The faithful will be able to appreciate more easily Mary's mission in the mystery of the Church and her pre-eminent place in the communion of saints if attention is drawn to the Second Vatican Council's references to the fundamental concepts of the nature of the Church as the Family of God, the People of God, the Kingdom of God and the Mystical Body of Christ.[86] This will also bring the faithful to a deeper realization of the brotherhood which unites all of them as sons and daughters of the Virgin Mary, "who with a mother's love has co-operated in their rebirth and spiritual forma-tion,"[87] and as sons and daughters of the Church, since "we are born from the Church's womb, we are nurtured by the Church's milk, we are given life by the Church's Spirit."[88] They will also realize that both the Church and Mary collaborate to give birth to the Mystical Body of Christ since "both of them are the Mother of Christ, but neither brings forth the whole [body] independently of the other."[89] Similarly the faithful will appreciate more clearly that the action of the Church in the world can be likened to an extension of Mary's concern. The active love she showed at Nazareth, in the house of Elizabeth, at Cana and on Golgotha—all salvific episodes having vast ecclesial importance—finds its extension in the Church's maternal concern that all men should come to knowledge of the truth (cf. 1 Tm. 2:4), in the Church's con-cern for people in lowly circumstances and for the poor and weak, and in her constant commit-ment to peace and social harmony, as well as in her untiring efforts to ensure that all men will share in the salvation which was merited for them by Christ's death. Thus love for the Church will become love for Mary, and vice versa, since

the one cannot exist without the other, as
St. Chromatius of Aquileia observed with keen
discernment: "The Church was united...in
the Upper Room with Mary the Mother of
Jesus and with His brethren. The Church therefore cannot be referred to as such unless it
includes Mary the Mother of our Lord, together
with His brethren." [90] In conclusion, therefore,
we repeat that devotion to the Blessed Virgin
must explicitly show its intrinsic and ecclesiological content: thus it will be enabled to
revise its forms and texts in a fitting way.

Section Two

FOUR GUIDELINES FOR DEVOTION TO THE BLESSED VIRGIN: BIBLICAL, LITURGICAL, ECUMENICAL AND ANTHROPOLOGICAL

29. The above considerations spring from
an examination of the Virgin Mary's relationship with God—the Father and the Son and
the Holy Spirit—and with the Church. Following the path traced by conciliar teaching,[91] we
wish to add some further guidelines from
Scripture, liturgy, ecumenism and anthro-
pology. These are to be borne in mind in any
revision of exercises of piety or in the creation
of new ones, in order to emphasize and accentu-
ate the bond which unites us to her who is the
Mother of Christ and our Mother in the communion of saints.

30. Today it is recognized as a general
need of Christian piety that every form of
worship should have a biblical imprint. The

progress made in biblical studies, the increasing dissemination of the Sacred Scriptures, and above all the example of Tradition and the interior action of the Holy Spirit are tending to cause the modern Christian to use the Bible ever increasingly as the basic prayerbook, and to draw from it genuine inspiration and unsurpassable examples. Devotion to the Blessed Virgin cannot be exempt from this general orientation of Christian piety[92]; indeed it should draw inspiration in a special way from this orientation in order to gain new vigor and sure help. In its wonderful presentation of God's plan for man's salvation, the Bible is replete with the mystery of the Savior, and from Genesis to the Book of Revelation, also contains clear references to her who was the Mother and associate of the Savior. We would not, however, wish this biblical imprint to be merely a diligent use of texts and symbols skillfully selected from the Sacred Scriptures. More than this is necessary. What is needed is that texts of prayers and chants should draw their inspiration and their wording from the Bible, and above all that devotion to the Virgin should be imbued with the great themes of the Christian message. This will ensure that, as they venerate the Seat of Wisdom, the faithful in their turn will be enlightened by the divine Word and be inspired to live their lives in accordance with the precepts of Incarnate Wisdom.

31. We have already spoken of the veneration which the Church gives to the Mother of God in the celebration of the sacred liturgy.

However, speaking of the other forms of devotion and of the criteria on which they should be based we wish to recall the norm laid down in the Constitution *Sacrosanctum concilium*. This document, while wholeheartedly approving of the practices of piety of the Christian people, goes on to say: "...it is necessary however that such devotions with consideration for the liturgical seasons should be so arranged as to be in harmony with the sacred liturgy. They should somehow derive their inspiration from it, and because of its pre-eminence they should orient the Christian people towards it."[93] Although this is a wise and clear rule, its application is not an easy matter, especially in regard to Marian devotions, which are so varied in their formal expressions. What is needed on the part of the leaders of the local communities is effort, pastoral sensitivity and perseverance, while the faithful on their part must show a willingness to accept guidelines and ideas drawn from the true nature of Christian worship; this sometimes makes it necessary to change long-standing customs wherein the real nature of this Christian worship has become somewhat obscured.

In this context we wish to mention two attitudes which in pastoral practice could nullify the norm of the Second Vatican Council. In the first place there are certain persons concerned with the care of souls who scorn, *a priori*, devotions of piety which, in their correct forms, have been recommended by the magisterium, who leave them aside and in this way create a vacuum which they do not fill. They forget that the Council has said that devotions of piety should harmonize with the liturgy, not be suppressed. Secondly there are those who, without wholesome liturgical and pastoral criteria, mix practices of piety and liturgical acts in hybrid celebrations. It sometimes happens that novenas or similar practices of piety are inserted into the very celebration of the Eucharistic Sacrifice. This creates the danger that the Lord's Memorial Rite, instead of being the culmination of the meeting of the Christian community, becomes the occasion, as it were, for devotional practices. For those who act in this way we wish to recall the rule laid down by the Council prescribing that exercises of piety should be harmonized with the liturgy, not merged into it. Wise pastoral action should, on the one hand, point out and emphasize the proper nature of the liturgical acts, while on the other hand it should enhance the value of practices of piety in order to adapt them to the needs of individual communities in the Church and to make them valuable aids to the liturgy.

32. Because of its ecclesial character, devotion to the Blessed Virgin reflects the preoccupations of the Church herself. Among these especially in our day is her anxiety for the re-establishment of Christian unity. In this way devotion to the Mother of the Lord is in accord with the deep desires and aims of the ecumenical movement, that is, it acquires an ecumenical aspect. This is so for a number of reasons.

In the first place, in venerating with particular love the glorious Theotokos and in acclaiming her as the "Hope of Christians," [94] Catholics unite themselves with their brethren of the Orthodox Churches, in which devotion to the Blessed Virgin finds its expression in a beautiful lyricism and in solid doctrine. Catholics are also united with Anglicans, whose classical theologians have already drawn attention to the sound scriptural basis for devotion to the Mother of our Lord, while those of the present day increasingly underline the importance of Mary's place in the Christian life. Praising God with the very words of the Virgin (cf. Lk. 1:46-55), they are united, too, with their brethren in the Churches of the Reform, where love for the Sacred Scriptures flourishes.

For Catholics, devotion to the Mother of Christ and Mother of Christians is also a natural and frequent opportunity for seeking her intercession with her Son in order to obtain the union of all the baptized within a single People of God.[95] Yet again, the ecumenical aspect of Marian devotion is shown in the Catholic Church's desire that, without in any way detracting from the unique character of this devotion,[96] every care should be taken to avoid any exaggeration which could mislead other Christian brethren about the true doctrine of the Catholic Church.[97] Similarly, the Church desires that any manifestation of cult which is opposed to correct Catholic practice should be eliminated.

Finally, since it is natural that in true devotion to the Blessed Virgin "the Son should be

duly known, loved and glorified ... when the
Mother is honored,"[98] such devotion is an approach to Christ, the source and center of ec-
clesiastical communion, in which all who
openly confess that He is God and Lord, Savior
and sole Mediator (cf. 1 Tm. 2:5) are called to
to be one, with one another, with Christ and
with the Father in the unity of the Holy Spirit.[99]

33. We realize that there exist important
differences between the thought of many of
our brethren in other Churches and ecclesial
communities and the Catholic doctrine on
"Mary's role in the work of salvation."[100] In
consequence there are likewise differences
of opinion on the devotion which should be
shown to her. Nevertheless, since it is the same
power of the Most High which overshadowed
the Virgin of Nazareth (cf. Lk. 1:35) and which
today is at work within the ecumenical movement and making it fruitful, we wish to express
our confidence that devotion to the humble
handmaid of the Lord, in whom the Almighty
has done great things (cf. Lk. 1:49), will become,
even if only slowly, not an obstacle but a path
and a rallying point for the union of all who
believe in Christ. We are glad to see that, in
fact, a better understanding of Mary's place in
the mystery of Christ and of the Church on the
part also of our separated brethren is smoothing
the path to union. Just as at Cana the Blessed
Virgin's intervention resulted in Christ's per-
forming His first miracle (cf. Jn. 2:1-12), so today
her intercession can help to bring to realization
the time when the disciples of Christ will again

find full communion in faith. This hope of ours is strengthened by a remark of our predecessor Leo XIII, who wrote that the cause of Christian unity "properly pertains to the role of Mary's spiritual motherhood. For Mary did not and cannot engender those who belong to Christ, except in one faith and one love: for 'Is Christ divided?' (1 Cor. 1:13) We must all live together the life of Christ, so that in one and the same body 'we may bear fruit for God' (Rom. 7:4)." [101]

34. Devotion to the Blessed Virgin must also pay close attention to certain findings of the human sciences. This will help to eliminate one of the causes of the difficulties experienced in devotion to the Mother of the Lord, namely, the discrepancy existing between some aspects of this devotion and modern anthropological discoveries and the profound changes which have occurred in the psycho-sociological field in which modern man lives and works. The picture of the Blessed Virgin presented in a certain type of devotional literature cannot easily be reconciled with today's lifestyle, especially the way women live today. In the home, woman's equality and co-responsibility with man in the running of the family are being justly recognized by laws and the evolution of customs. In the sphere of politics women have in many countries gained a position in public life equal to that of men. In the social field women are at work in a whole range of different employments, getting further away every day from the restricted surroundings of the home. In the cultural field new possibilities

are opening up for women in scientific research and intellectual activities.

In consequence of these phenomena some people are becoming disenchanted with devotion to the Blessed Virgin and finding it difficult to take as an example Mary of Nazareth because the horizons of her life, so they say, seem rather restricted in comparison with the vast spheres of activity open to mankind today. In this regard we exhort theologians, those responsible for the local Christian communities and the faithful themselves to examine these difficulties with due care. At the same time we wish to take the opportunity of offering our own contribution to their solution by making a few observations.

35. First, the Virgin Mary has always been proposed to the faithful by the Church as an example to be imitated, not precisely in the type of life she led, and much less for the socio-cultural background in which she lived and which today scarcely exists anywhere. She is held up as an example to the faithful rather for the way in which, in her own particular life, she fully and responsibly accepted the will of God (cf. Lk. 1:38), because she heard the word of God and acted on it, and because charity and a spirit of service were the driving force of her actions. She is worthy of imitation because she was the first and the most perfect of Christ's disciples. All of this has a permanent and universal exemplary value.

36. Secondly, we would like to point out that the difficulties alluded to above are closely

related to certain aspects of the image of Mary
found in popular writings. They are not connected with the Gospel image of Mary nor with
the doctrinal data which have been made explicit
through a slow and conscientious process of
drawing from Revelation. It should be considered quite normal for succeeding generations
of Christians in differing socio-cultural contexts
to have expressed their sentiments about the
Mother of Jesus in a way and manner which
reflected their own age. In contemplating Mary
and her mission these different generations
of Christians, looking on her as the New Woman
and perfect Christian, found in her as a virgin,
wife and mother the outstanding type of woman-
hood and the pre-eminent exemplar of life lived
in accordance with the Gospels and summing
up the most characteristic situations in the life
of a woman. When the Church considers the
long history of Marian devotion she rejoices at
the continuity of the element of cult which it
shows, but she does not bind herself to any particular expression of an individual cultural
epoch or to the particular anthropological ideas
underlying such expressions. The Church
understands that certain outward religious
expressions, while perfectly valid in themselves,
may be less suitable to men and women of different ages and cultures.

37. Finally, we wish to point out that our
own time, no less than former times, is called
upon to verify its knowledge of reality with the
word of God, and, keeping to the matter at present under consideration, to compare its an-

thropological ideas and the problems springing
therefrom with the figure of the Virgin Mary
as presented by the Gospel. The reading of the
divine Scriptures, carried out under the guidance
of the Holy Spirit, and with the discoveries of
the human sciences and the different situations
in the world today being taken into account,
will help us to see how Mary can be considered
a mirror of the expectations of the men and
women of our time. Thus, the modern woman,
anxious to participate with decision-making
power in the affairs of the community, will
contemplate with intimate joy Mary who, taken
into dialogue with God, gives her active and
responsible consent,[102] not to the solution of
a contingent problem, but to that "event of
world importance," as the Incarnation of the
Word has been rightly called.[103] The modern
woman will appreciate that Mary's choice of the
state of virginity, which in God's plan prepared
her for the mystery of the Incarnation, was not
a rejection of any of the values of the married
state but a courageous choice which she made
in order to consecrate herself totally to the love
of God. The modern woman will note with
pleasant surprise that Mary of Nazareth, while
completely devoted to the will of God, was far
from being a timidly submissive woman or one
whose piety was repellent to others; on the contrary, she was a woman who did not hesitate
to proclaim that God vindicates the humble
and the oppressed, and removes the powerful
people of this world from their privileged posi-
tions (cf. Lk. 1:51-53). The modern woman will

recognize in Mary, who "stands out among the poor and humble of the Lord," [104] a woman of strength, who experienced poverty and suffering, flight and exile (cf. Mt. 2:13-23). These are situations that cannot escape the attention of those who wish to support, with the Gospel spirit, the liberating energies of man and of society. And Mary will appear not as a Mother exclusively concerned with her own divine Son, but rather as a woman whose action helped to strengthen the apostolic community's faith in Christ (cf. Jn. 2:1-12), and whose maternal role was extended and became universal on Calvary. [105] These are but examples, but examples which show clearly that the figure of the Blessed Virgin does not disillusion any of the profound expectations of the men and women of our time but offers them the perfect model of the disciple of the Lord: the disciple who builds up the earthly and temporal city while being a diligent pilgrim towards the heavenly and eternal city; the disciple who works for that justice which sets free the oppressed and for that charity which assists the needy; but above all, the disciple who is the active witness of that love which builds up Christ in people's hearts.

38. Having offered these directives, which are intended to favor the harmonious development of devotion to the Mother of the Lord, we consider it opportune to draw attention to certain attitudes of piety which are incorrect. The Second Vatican Council has already authoritatively denounced both the exaggeration of content and form which even falsifies doctrine

and likewise the small-mindedness which obscures the figure and mission of Mary. The Council has also denounced certain devotional deviations, such as vain credulity, which substitutes reliance on merely external practices for serious commitment. Another deviation is sterile and ephemeral sentimentality, so alien to the spirit of the Gospel that demands persevering and practical action.[106] We reaffirm the Council's reprobation of such attitudes and practices. They are not in harmony with the Catholic Faith and therefore they must have no place in Catholic worship. Careful defense against these errors and deviations will render devotion to the Blessed Virgin more vigorous and more authentic. It will make this devotion solidly based, with the consequence that study of the sources of Revelation and attention to the documents of the magisterium will prevail over the exaggerated search for novelties or extraordinary phenomena. It will ensure that this devotion is objective in its historical setting, and for this reason everything that is obviously legendary or false must be eliminated. It will ensure that this devotion matches its doctrinal content — hence the necessity of avoiding a one-sided presentation of the figure of Mary, which by overstressing one element compromises the overall picture given by the Gospel. It will make this devotion clear in its motivation; hence every unworthy self-interest is to be carefully banned from the area of what is sacred.

39. Finally, insofar as it may be necessary we would like to repeat that the ultimate purpose

of devotion to the Blessed Virgin is to glorify
God and to lead Christians to commit themselves
to a life which is in absolute conformity with
His will. When the children of the Church
unite their voices with the voice of the unknown
woman in the Gospel and glorify the Mother of
Jesus by saying to Him: "Blessed is the womb
that bore you and the breasts that you sucked"
(Lk. 11:27), they will be led to ponder the Divine
Master's serious reply: "Blessed rather are those
who hear the word of God and keep it!" (Lk.
11:28) While it is true that this reply is in itself
lively praise of Mary, as various Fathers of the
Church interpreted it[107] and the Second Vatican
Council has confirmed,[108] it is also an admonition
to us to live our lives in accordance with God's
commandments. It is also an echo of other
words of the Savior: "Not everyone who says
to me 'Lord, Lord,' will enter the kingdom of
heaven" (Mt. 7:21); and again: "You are my
friends if you do what I command you" (Jn.
15:14).

PART THREE

Observations on Two Exercises of Piety: the Angelus and the Rosary

40. We have indicated a number of principles which can help to give fresh vigor to devotion to the Mother of the Lord. It is now up to episcopal conferences, to those in charge of local communities and to the various religious congregations prudently to revise practices and exercises of piety in honor of the Blessed Virgin, and to encourage the creative impulse of those who through genuine religious inspiration or pastoral sensitivity wish to establish new forms of piety. For different reasons we nevertheless feel it is opportune to consider here two practices which are widespread in the West, and with which this Apostolic See has concerned itself on various occasions: the Angelus and the rosary.

THE ANGELUS

41. What we have to say about the Angelus is meant to be only a simple but earnest ex-

hortation to continue its traditional recitation wherever and whenever possible. The Angelus does not need to be revised, because of its simple structure, its biblical character, its historical origin which links it to the prayer for peace and safety, and its quasi-liturgical rhythm which sanctifies different moments during the day, and because it reminds us of the Paschal Mystery, in which recalling the Incarnation of the Son of God we pray that we may be led "through his passion and cross to the glory of his resurrection." [109] These factors ensure that the Angelus despite the passing of centuries retains an unaltered value and an intact freshness. It is true that certain customs traditionally linked with the recitation of the Angelus have disappeared or can continue only with difficulty in modern life. But these are marginal elements. The value of contemplation on the mystery of the Incarnation of the Word, of the greeting to the Virgin, and of recourse to her merciful intercession remains unchanged. And despite the changed conditions of the times, for the majority of people there remain unaltered the characteristic periods of the day — morning, noon and evening — which mark the periods of their activity and constitute an invitation to pause in prayer.

THE ROSARY

42. We wish now, venerable brothers, to dwell for a moment on the renewal of the pious practice which has been called "the com-

pendium of the entire Gospel"[110]: the rosary. To this our predecessors have devoted close attention and care. On many occasions they have recommended its frequent recitation, encouraged its diffusion, explained its nature, recognized its suitability for fostering contemplative prayer—prayer of both praise and petition—and recalled its intrinsic effectiveness for promoting Christian life and apostolic commitment.

We, too, from the first general audience of our pontificate on July 13, 1963, have shown our great esteem for the pious practice of the rosary.[111] Since that time we have underlined its value on many different occasions, some ordinary, some grave. Thus, at a moment of anguish and uncertainty, we published the letter *Christi Matri* (September 15, 1966), in order to obtain prayers to our Lady of the Rosary and to implore from God the supreme benefit of peace.[112] We renewed this appeal in our Apostolic Exhortation *Recurrens mensis October* (October 7, 1969), in which we also commemorated the fourth centenary of the Apostolic Letter *Consueverunt Romani pontifices* of our predecessor St. Pius V, who in that document explained and in a certain sense established the traditional form of the rosary.[113]

43. Our assiduous and affectionate interest in the rosary has led us to follow very attentively the numerous meetings which in recent years have been devoted to the pastoral role of the rosary in the modern world, meetings arranged by associations and individuals profoundly attached to the rosary and attended by bishops,

priests, religious and lay people of proven experience and recognized ecclesial awareness. Among these people special mention should be made of the sons of St. Dominic, by tradition the guardians and promoters of this very salutary practice. Parallel with such meetings has been the research work of historians, work aimed not at defining in a sort of archaeological fashion the primitive form of the rosary but at uncovering the original inspiration and driving force behind it and its essential structure. The fundamental characteristics of the rosary, its essential elements and their mutual relationship have all emerged more clearly from these congresses and from the research carried out.

44. Thus, for instance, the Gospel inspiration of the rosary has appeared more clearly: the rosary draws from the Gospel the presentation of the mysteries and its main formulas. As it moves from the angel's joyful greeting and the Virgin's pious assent, the rosary takes its inspiration from the Gospel to suggest the attitude with which the faithful should recite it. In the harmonious succession of *Hail Marys* the rosary puts before us once more a fundamental mystery of the Gospel—the Incarnation of the Word, contemplated at the decisive moment of the Annunciation to Mary. The rosary is thus a Gospel prayer, as pastors and scholars like to define it, more today perhaps than in the past.

45. It has also been more easily seen how the orderly and gradual unfolding of the rosary reflects the very way in which the Word of God,

mercifully entering into human affairs, brought
about the Redemption. The rosary considers
in harmonious succession the principal salvific
events accomplished in Christ, from His virginal
conception and the mysteries of His childhood
to the culminating moments of the Passover—the
blessed passion and the glorious resurrection—
and to the effects of this on the infant Church
on the day of Pentecost, and on the Virgin Mary
when at the end of her earthly life she was
assumed body and soul into her heavenly home.
It has also been observed that the division of the
mysteries of the rosary into three parts not only
adheres strictly to the chronological order of
the facts but above all reflects the plan of the
original proclamation of the Faith and sets forth
once more the mystery of Christ in the very
way in which it is seen by St. Paul in the celebrated "hymn" of the Letter to the Philip-
pians—kenosis, death and exaltation (cf. 2:6-11).

46. As a Gospel prayer, centered on the
mystery of the redemptive Incarnation, the
rosary is therefore a prayer with a clearly Christological orientation. Its most characteristic
element, in fact, the litany-like succession of
Hail Marys, becomes in itself an unceasing
praise of Christ, who is the ultimate object both
of the angel's announcement and of the greeting
of the mother of John the Baptist: "Blessed is
the fruit of your womb" (Lk. 1:42). We would go
further and say that the succession of *Hail
Marys* constitutes the warp on which is woven
the contemplation of the mysteries. The Jesus
that each *Hail Mary* recalls is the same Jesus

whom the succession of the mysteries proposes to us—now as the Son of God, now as the Son of the Virgin—at His birth in a stable at Bethlehem, at His presentation by His Mother in the Temple, as a youth full of zeal for His Father's affairs, as the Redeemer in agony in the garden, scourged and crowned with thorns, carrying the cross and dying on Calvary; risen from the dead and ascended to the glory of the Father to send forth the gift of the Spirit. As is well known, at one time there was a custom, still preserved in certain places, of adding to the name of Jesus in each *Hail Mary* a reference to the mystery being contemplated. And this was done precisely in order to help contemplation and to make the mind and the voice act in unison.

47. There has also been felt with greater urgency the need to point out once more the importance of a further essential element in the rosary, in addition to the value of the elements of praise and petition, namely the element of contemplation. Without this the rosary is a body without a soul, and its recitation is in danger of becoming a mechanical repetition of formulas and of going counter to the warning of Christ: "And in praying do not heap up empty phrases as the Gentiles do; for they think that they will be heard for their many words" (Mt. 6:7). By its nature the recitation of the rosary calls for a quiet rhythm and a lingering pace, helping the individual to meditate on the mysteries of the Lord's life as seen through the eyes of her who was closest to the Lord. In this way the

unfathomable riches of these mysteries are un-
folded.

48. Finally, as a result of modern reflection
the relationships between the liturgy and the
rosary have been more clearly understood.
On the one hand it has been emphasized that
the rosary is, as it were, a branch sprung from
the ancient trunk of the Christian liturgy, the
Psalter of the Blessed Virgin, whereby the humble were associated in the Church's hymn of
praise and universal intercession. On the other
hand it has been noted that this development
occurred at a time—the last period of the Middle Ages—when the liturgical spirit was in
decline and the faithful were turning from the
liturgy towards a devotion to Christ's humanity
and to the Blessed Virgin Mary, a devotion favoring a certain external sentiment of piety. Not
many years ago some people began to express
the desire to see the rosary included among the
rites of the liturgy, while other people, anxious
to avoid repetition of former pastoral mistakes,
unjustifiably disregarded the rosary. Today the
problem can easily be solved in the light of the
principles of the Constitution *Sacrosanctum
concilium.* Liturgical celebrations and the pious
practice of the rosary must be neither set in
opposition to one another nor considered as
being identical.[114] The more an expression of
prayer preserves its own true nature and individual characteristics the more fruitful it becomes. Once the pre-eminent value of liturgical
rites has been reaffirmed it will not be difficult
to appreciate the fact that the rosary is a prac-

tice of piety which easily harmonizes with the liturgy. In fact, like the liturgy, it is of a community nature, draws its inspiration from Sacred Scripture and is oriented towards the mystery of Christ. The commemoration in the liturgy and the contemplative remembrance proper to the rosary, although existing on essentially different planes of reality, have as their object the same salvific events wrought by Christ. The former presents anew, under the veil of signs and operative in a hidden way, the great mysteries of our Redemption. The latter, by means of devout contemplation, recalls these same mysteries to the mind of the person praying and stimulates the will to draw from them the norms of living. Once this substantial difference has been established, it is not difficult to understand that the rosary is an exercise of piety that draws its motivating force from the liturgy and leads naturally back to it, if practiced in conformity with its original inspiration. It does not, however, become part of the liturgy. In fact, meditation on the mysteries of the rosary, by familiarizing the hearts and minds of the faithful with the mysteries of Christ, can be an excellent preparation for the celebration of those same mysteries in the liturgical action and can also become a continuing echo thereof. However, it is a mistake to recite the rosary during the celebration of the liturgy, though unfortunately this practice still persists here and there.

49. The rosary of the Blessed Virgin Mary, according to the tradition accepted by our predecessor St. Pius V and authoritatively taught

by him, consists of various elements disposed in an organic fashion:

a) Contemplation in communion with Mary, of a series of *mysteries of salvation*, wisely distributed into three cycles. These mysteries express the joy of the messianic times, the salvific suffering of Christ and the glory of the Risen Lord which fills the Church. This contemplation by its very nature encourages practical reflection and provides stimulating norms for living.

b) The Lord's Prayer, or *Our Father*, which by reason of its immense value is at the basis of Christian prayer and ennobles that prayer in its various expressions.

c) The litany-like succession of the *Hail Mary*, which is made up of the angel's greeting to the Virgin (cf. Lk. 1:28), and of Elizabeth's greeting (cf. Lk. 1:42), followed by the ecclesial supplication, *Holy Mary.* The continued series of *Hail Marys* is the special characteristic of the rosary, and their number, in the full and typical number of one hundred and fifty, presents a certain analogy with the Psalter and is an element that goes back to the very origin of the exercise of piety. But this number, divided, according to a well-tried custom, into decades attached to the individual mysteries, is distributed in the three cycles already mentioned, thus giving rise to the rosary of fifty *Hail Marys* as we know it. This latter has entered into use as the normal measure of the pious exercise and as such has been adopted by popular piety and approved by papal authority, which also enriched it with numerous indulgences.

d) The doxology *Glory be to the Father* which, in conformity with an orientation common to Christian piety, concludes the prayer with the glorifying of God who is one and three, from whom, through whom and in whom all things have their being (cf. Rom. 11:36).

50. These are the elements of the rosary. Each has its own particular character which, wisely understood and appreciated, should be reflected in the recitation in order that the rosary may express all its richness and variety. Thus the recitation will be grave and suppliant during the Lord's Prayer, lyrical and full of praise during the tranquil succession of *Hail Marys*, contemplative in the recollected meditation on the mysteries and full of adoration during the doxology. This applies to all the ways in which the rosary is usually recited: privately, in intimate recollection with the Lord; in community, in the family or in groups of the faithful gathered together to ensure the special presence of the Lord (cf. Mt. 18:20); or publicly, in assemblies to which the ecclesial community is invited.

51. In recent times certain exercises of piety have been created which take their inspiration from the rosary. Among such exercises we wish to draw attention to and recommend those which insert into the ordinary celebration of the word of God some elements of the rosary, such as meditation on the mysteries and litany-like repetition of the angel's greeting to Mary.

In this way these elements gain in importance, since they are found in the context of Bible readings, illustrated with a homily, accompanied by silent pauses and emphasized with song. We are happy to know that such practices have helped to promote a more complete understanding of the spiritual riches of the rosary itself and have served to restore esteem for its recitation among youth associations and movements.

52. We now desire, as a continuation of the thought of our predecessors, to recommend strongly the recitation of the family rosary. The Second Vatican Council has pointed out how the family, the primary and vital cell of society, "shows itself to be the domestic sanctuary of the Church through the mutual affection of its members and the common prayer they offer to God." [115] The Christian family is thus seen to be a domestic Church [116] if its members, each according to his proper place and tasks, all together promote justice, practice works of mercy, devote themselves to helping their brethren, take part in the apostolate of the wider local community and play their part in its liturgical worship. [117] This will be all the more true if together they offer up prayers to God. If this element of common prayer were missing, the family would lack its very character as a domestic Church. Thus there must logically follow a concrete effort to reinstate communal prayer in family life if there is to be a restoration of the theological concept of the family as the domestic Church.

53. In accordance with the directives of the Council, the *Institutio Generalis de Liturgia Horarum* rightly numbers the family among the groups in which the Divine Office can suitably be celebrated in community: "It is fitting... that the family, as a domestic sanctuary of the Church, should not only offer prayers to God in common, but also, according to circumstances, should recite parts of the Liturgy of the Hours, in order to be more intimately linked with the Church."[118] No avenue should be left unexplored to ensure that this clear and practical recommendation finds within Christian families growing and joyful acceptance.

54. But there is no doubt that, after the celebration of the Liturgy of the Hours, the high point which family prayer can reach, the rosary should be considered as one of the best and most efficacious prayers in common that the Christian family is invited to recite. We like to think, and sincerely hope, that when the family gathering becomes a time of prayer, the rosary is a frequent and favored manner of praying. We are well aware that the changed conditions of life today do not make family gatherings easy, and that even when such a gathering is possible many circumstances make it difficult to turn it into an occasion of prayer. There is no doubt of the difficulty. But it is characteristic of the Christian in his manner of life not to give in to circumstances but to overcome them, not to succumb but to make an effort. Families which want to live in full measure the vocation and spirituality proper to the Christian family must

therefore devote all their energies to overcoming the pressures that hinder family gatherings and prayer in common.

55. In concluding these observations, which give proof of the concern and esteem which the Apostolic See has for the rosary of the Blessed Virgin, we desire at the same time to recommend that this very worthy devotion should not be propagated in a way that is too one-sided or exclusive. The rosary is an excellent prayer, but the faithful should feel serenely free in its regard. They should be drawn to its calm recitation by its intrinsic appeal.

CONCLUSION

Theological and Pastoral Value of Devotion to the Blessed Virgin

56. Venerable brothers, as we come to the end of this our Apostolic Exhortation we wish to sum up and emphasize the theological value of devotion to the Blessed Virgin and to recall briefly its pastoral effectiveness for renewing the Christian way of life.

The Church's devotion to the Blessed Virgin is an intrinsic element of Christian worship. The honor which the Church has always and everywhere shown to the Mother of the Lord, from the blessing with which Elizabeth greeted Mary (cf. Lk. 1:42-45) right up to the expressions of praise and petition used today, is a very strong witness to the Church's norm of prayer and an invitation to become more deeply conscious of her norm of faith. And the converse is likewise true. The Church's norm of faith requires that her norm of prayer should everywhere blossom forth with regard to the Mother of Christ. Such devotion to the Blessed Virgin is firmly rooted in the revealed word and has solid dogmatic foundations. It is based on the singular dignity of Mary, "Mother of the Son of God, and therefore beloved daughter of the Father and Temple of the Holy Spirit — Mary, who, because of this extraordinary grace, is far greater than any other creature on earth or in heaven." [119] This devotion takes into account the part she played at decisive moments in the history of the salvation which her Son accomplished, and her holiness, already full at her Immaculate Conception yet increasing all the time as she obeyed the will of the Father and accepted the path of suffering (cf. Lk. 2:34-35, 41-52; Jn. 19:25-27), growing constantly in faith, hope and charity. Devotion to Mary recalls too her mission and the special position she holds within the People of God, of which she is the preeminent member, a shining example and the loving Mother; it recalls her unceasing and efficacious intercession which, although she is assumed into heaven, draws her close to those who ask her help, including those who do not realize that they are her children. It recalls Mary's glory which ennobles the whole of mankind, as the outstanding phrase of Dante recalls: "You have so ennobled human nature that its very Creator did not disdain to share in it." [120] Mary, in fact, is one of our race, a true daughter of Eve — though free of that mother's sin — and truly our sister, who as a poor and humble woman fully shared our lot.

We would add further that devotion to the Blessed Virgin finds its ultimate justification in the unfathomable and free will of God who, being eternal and divine charity (cf. 1 Jn. 4:7-8, 16), accomplishes all things according to a loving design. He loved her and did great things for her (cf. Lk. 1:49). He loved her for His own sake, and He loved her for our sake, too; He gave her to Himself and He gave her also to us.

57. Christ is the only way to the Father (cf. Jn. 14:4-11), and the ultimate example to whom the disciple must conform his own conduct (cf. Jn. 13:15), to the extent of sharing Christ's sentiments (cf. Phil. 2:5), living His life and possessing His Spirit (cf. Gal. 2:20; Rom. 8:10-11). The Church has always taught this and nothing in pastoral activity should obscure this doctrine. But the Church, taught by the Holy Spirit and benefiting from centuries of experience, recognizes that devotion to the Blessed Virgin, subordinated to worship of the divine Savior and in connection with it, also has a great pastoral effectiveness and constitutes a force for renewing Christian living. It is easy to see the reason for this effectiveness. Mary's many-sided mission to the People of God is a supernatural reality which operates and bears fruit within the body of the Church. One finds cause for joy in considering the different aspects of this mission, and seeing how each of these aspects with its individual effectiveness is directed towards the same end, namely, producing in the children

the spiritual characteristics of the first-born Son. The Virgin's maternal intercession, her exemplary holiness and the divine grace which is in her become for the human race a reason for divine hope.

The Blessed Virgin's role as Mother leads the People of God to turn with filial confidence to her who is ever ready to listen with a mother's affection and efficacious assistance.[121] Thus the People of God have learned to call on her as the Consoler of the afflicted, the Health of the sick, and the Refuge of sinners, that they may find comfort in tribulation, relief in sickness and liberating strength in guilt. For she, who is free from sin, leads her children to combat sin with energy and resoluteness.[122] This liberation from sin and evil (cf. Mt. 6:13) — it must be repeated — is the necessary premise for any renewal of Christian living.

The Blessed Virgin's exemplary holiness encourages the faithful to "raise their eyes to Mary who shines forth before the whole community of the elect as a model of the virtues."[123] It is a question of solid, evangelical virtues: faith and the docile acceptance of the Word of God (cf. Lk. 1:26-38, 1:45, 11:27-28; Jn. 2:5); generous obedience (cf. Lk. 1:38); genuine humility (cf. Lk. 1:48); solicitous charity (cf. Lk. 1:39-56); profound wisdom (cf. Lk. 1:29, 34; 2:19, 33:51); worship of God manifested in alacrity in the fulfillment of religious duties (cf. Lk. 2:21-41), in gratitude for the gifts received (cf. Lk. 1:46-49), in her offering in the Temple (cf. Lk. 2:22-24) and in her prayer in the midst of the apostolic community (cf. Acts 1:12-14); her fortitude in exile (cf. Mt. 2:13-23) and in suffering (cf. Lk. 2:34-35, 49; Jn. 19:25); her poverty reflecting dignity and trust in God (cf. Lk. 1:48, 2:24); her attentive care for her Son, from His humble birth to the ignominy of the cross (cf. Lk. 2:1-7; Jn. 19:25-27); her delicate forethought (cf. Jn. 2:1-11); her virginal purity (cf. Mt. 1:18-25; Lk. 1:26-38); her strong and chaste married love. These virtues of the Mother will also adorn her children who steadfastly study her example in order to reflect it in their own lives. And this progress in virtue will appear as the consequence and the already mature fruit of that pastoral zeal which springs from devotion to the Blessed Virgin.

Devotion to the Mother of the Lord becomes for the faithful an opportunity for growing in divine grace, and this is the ultimate aim of all pastoral activity. For it is impossible to honor her who is "full of grace" (Lk. 1:28) without thereby honoring in oneself the state of grace, which is friendship with God, communion with Him and the indwelling of the Holy Spirit. It is this divine grace which takes possession of the whole man and conforms him to the image of the Son of God (cf. Rom. 8:29; Col. 1:18). The Catholic Church, endowed with centuries of experience, recognizes in devotion to the Blessed Virgin a powerful aid for man as he strives for fulfillment. Mary, the New

Woman, stands at the side of Christ, the New Man, within whose mystery the mystery of man[124] alone finds true light; she is given to us as a pledge and guarantee that God's plan in Christ for the salvation of the whole man has already achieved realization in a creature: in her. Contemplated in the episodes of the Gospels and in the reality which she already possesses in the City of God, the Blessed Virgin Mary offers a calm vision and a reassuring word to modern man, torn as he often is between anguish and hope, defeated by the sense of his own limitations and assailed by limitless aspirations, troubled in his mind and divided in his heart, uncertain before the riddle of death, oppressed by loneliness while yearning for fellowship, a prey to boredom and disgust. She shows forth the victory of hope over anguish, of fellowship over solitude, of peace over anxiety, of joy and beauty over boredom and disgust, of eternal visions over earthly ones, of life over death.

Let the very words that she spoke to the servants at the marriage feast of Cana, "Do whatever he tells you" (Jn. 2:5), be a seal on our exhortation and a further reason in favor of the pastoral value of devotion to the Blessed Virgin as a means of leading men to Christ. Those words, which at first sight were limited to the desire to remedy an embarrassment at the feast, are seen in the context of St. John's Gospel to reecho the words used by the people of Israel to give approval to the Covenant at Sinai (cf. Ex. 19:8, 24:3, 7; Dt. 5:27) and to renew their commitments (cf. Jos. 24:24; Ezr.

10:12; Neh. 5:12). And they are words which harmonize wonderfully with those spoken by the Father at the theophany on Mount Tabor: "Listen to him" (Mt. 17:5).

EPILOGUE

58. Venerable Brothers, we have dealt at length with an integral element of Christian worship: devotion to the Mother of the Lord. This has been called for by the nature of the subject, one which in these recent years has been the object of study and revision and at times the cause of some perplexity. We are consoled to think that the work done by this Apostolic See and by yourselves in order to carry out the norms of the Council — particularly the liturgical reform — is a steppingstone to an ever more lively and adoring worship of God, the Father and the Son and the Holy Spirit, and to an increase of the Christian life of the faithful. We are filled with confidence when we note that the renewed Roman liturgy, also taken as a whole, is a splendid illustration of the Church's devotion to the Blessed Virgin. We are upheld by the hope that the directives issued in order to render this devotion ever more pure and vigorous will be applied with sincerity. We rejoice that the Lord has given us the opportunity of putting forward some points for reflection in order to renew and confirm esteem for the practice of the rosary. Comfort, confidence, hope and joy are the sentiments which we wish to transform into fervent praise and thanksgiving to the Lord as we unite our voice

with that of the Blessed Virgin in accordance with the prayer of the Roman Liturgy.[125]

Dear Brothers, while we express the hope that, thanks to your generous commitment, there will be among the clergy and among the people entrusted to your care a salutary increase of devotion to Mary with undoubted profit for the Church and for society, we cordially impart our special apostolic blessing to yourselves and to all the faithful people to whom you devote your pastoral zeal.

Given in Rome, at St. Peter's, on the second day of February, the Feast of the Presentation of the Lord, in the year 1974, the eleventh of our pontificate.

1. Cf. Lactantius, *Divinae Institutiones* IV, 3, 6-10: *CSEL* 19, p. 279.

2. Cf. Second Vatican Council, Constitution on the Sacred Liturgy, *Sacrosanctum Concilium*, 1-3, 11, 21, 48. *AAS* 56 (1964), pp. 97-98, 102-103, 105-106, 113.

3. Second Vatican Council, Constitution on the Sacred Liturgy, *Sacrosanctum Concilium*, 103: *AAS* 56 (1964), p. 125.

4. Cf. Second Vatican Council, Dogmatic Constitution on the Church, *Lumen Gentium*, 66: *AAS* 57 (1965), p. 65.

5. *Ibid.*

6. Votive Mass of the Blessed Virgin Mary, Mother of the Church, Preface.

7. Cf. Second Vatican Council, Dogmatic Constitution on the Church, *Lumen Gentium*, 66-67: *AAS* 57 (1965),

pp. 65-66; Constitution on the Sacred Liturgy, *Sacrosanctum Concilium*, 103: *AAS* 56 (1964), p. 125.

8. Apostolic Exhortation, *Signum Magnum: AAS* 59 (1967), pp.. 465-475.

9. Cf. Second Vatican Council, Constitution on the Sacred Liturgy, *Sacrosanctum Concilium*, 3: *AAS* 56 (1964), p. 98.

10. Cf. Second Vatican Council, *ibid.*, 102: *AAS* 56 (1964), p. 125.

11. Cf. Roman Missal restored by Decree of the Sacred Ecumenical Second Vatican Council, promulgated by authority of Pope Paul VI, typical edition, MCMLXX, December 8, Preface.

12. Roman Missal, restored by Decree of the Sacred Ecumenical Second Vatican Council promulgated by authority of Pope Paul VI. *Ordo Lectionum Missae*, typical edition, MCMLXIX, p. 8. First Reading (Year A: Is. 7:10-14: "Behold a virgin shall conceive"; Year B: 2 Sam. 7:1-15; 8b-11, 16: "The throne of David shall be established for ever before the face of the Lord"; Year C: Mic. 5:2-5a [Heb. 1-4a]: "Out of you will be born for me the one who is to rule over Israel").

13. *Ibid.*, p. 8, Gospel (Year A: Mt. 1:18-24: "Jesus is born of Mary who was espoused to Joseph, the son of David"; Year B: Lk. 1:26-38: "You are to conceive and bear a son"; Year C: Lk. 1:39-45: "Why should I be honored with a visit from the mother of my Lord?").

14. Cf. Roman Missal, Advent Preface, II.

15. Cf. Roman Missal, *ibid.*

16. Roman Missal, Eucharistic Prayer I, *Communicantes* for Christmas and its octave.

17. Roman Missal, January 1, Entry antiphon and Collect.

18. Cf. Roman Missal, August 22, Collect.

19. Roman Missal, September 8, Prayer after Communion.

20. Roman Missal, May 31, Collect.

21. Cf. *ibid.*, Collect and Prayer over the gifts.

22. Cf. Roman Missal, September 15, Collect.

23. Cf. 1, p. 15.

24. From among the many anaphoras cf. the following which are held in special honor by the Eastern rites: *Anaphora Marci Evangelistae: Prex Eucharistica*, ed. A. Hänggi-I. Pahl, Fribourg, *Editions Universitaires*, 1968, p. 107; *Anaphora Iacobi fratris Domini graeca, ibid.*, p. 257; *Anaphora Ioannis Chrysostomi, ibid.*, p. 229.

25. Cf. Roman Missal, December 8, Preface.

26. Cf. Roman Missal, August 15, Preface.

27. Cf. Roman Missal, January 1, Prayer after Communion.

28. Cf. Roman Missal, Common of the Blessed Virgin Mary, 6, Paschaltide, Collect.

29. Roman Missal, September 15, Collect.

30. Roman Missal, May 31, Collect. On the same lines is the Preface of the Blessed Virgin Mary, II: "We do well... in celebrating the memory of the Virgin Mary... to glorify your love for us in the words of her song of thanksgiving."

31. Cf. Lectionary, III Sunday of Advent (Year C: Zeph. 3:14-18a); IV Sunday of Advent (cf. above footnote 12); Sunday within the octave of Christmas (Year A: Mt. 2:13-15; 19-23; Year B: Lk. 2:22-40; Year C: Lk. 2:41-52); II Sunday after Christmas (Jn. 1:1-18); VII Sunday after Easter (Year A: Acts 1:12-14); II Sunday of the Year (Year C: Jn. 1:1-12); X Sunday of the Year (Year B: Gen. 3:9-15); XIV Sunday of the Year (Year B: Mk. 6:1-6).

32. Cf. Lectionary, the catechumenate and baptism of adults; the Lord's Prayer (Second Reading, 2, Gal. 4:4-7); Christian initiation outside the Easter Vigil (Gospel, 7, Jn. 1:1-5; 9-14; 16-18); Nuptial Mass (Gospel, 7, Jn. 2:1-11); Consecration of Virgins and religious profession (First Reading, 7, Is. 61:9-11; Gospel, 6, Mk. 3:31-35; Lk. 1:26-38 [cf. *Ordo Consecrationis Virginum*, 130; *Ordo professionis religiosae, Pars altera*, 145]).

33. Cf. Lectionary, For refugees and exiles (Gospel, 1, Mt. 2:13-15; 19-23); In thanksgiving (First Reading, 4, Zeph. 3:14-15).

34. Cf. *La Divina Commedia, Paradiso XXXIII*, 1-9; cf. Liturgy of the Hours, remembrance of our Lady on Saturdays, Office of Reading, Hymn.

35. *Ordo baptismi parvulorum*, 48: *Ordo initiationis christianae adultorum*, 214.

36. Cf. *Rituale Romanum, Tit. VII, cap. III, De benedictione mulieris post partum.*

37. Cf. *Ordo professionis religiosae, Pars Prior*, 57 and 67.

38. Cf. *Ordo consecrationis virginum*, 16.

39. Cf. *Ordo professionis religiosae, Pars Prior*, 62 and 142; *Pars Altera*, 67 and 158; *Ordo consecrationis virginum*, 18 and 20.

40. Cf. *Ordo unctionis infirmorum eorumque pastoralis curae*, 143, 146, 147, 150.

41. Cf. Roman Missal, Masses for the Dead, For dead brothers and sisters, relations and benefactors, Collect.

42. Cf. *Ordo exsequiarum*, 226.

43. Cf. Second Vatican Council, Dogmatic Constitution on the Church, *Lumen Gentium*, 63: AAS 57 (1965), p. 64.

44. Cf. Second Vatican Council, Constitution on the Sacred Liturgy, *Sacrosanctum Concilium*, 7: AAS 56 (1964), pp. 100-101.

45. *Sermo* 215, 4: *PL* 38, 1074.

46. *Ibid.*

47. Cf. Second Vatican Council, Dogmatic Constitution on Divine Revelation, *Dei Verbum*, 21: AAS 58 (1966), pp. 827-828.

48. Cf. *Adversus Haereses* IV, 7, 1: *PG* 7, 1, 990-991; *S. Ch.* 100, t. II, pp. 454-458.

49. Cf. *Adversus Haereses* III, 10, 2: *PG* 7, 1, 873; *S. Ch.* 34, p. 164.

50. Cf. Second Vatican Council, Dogmatic Constitution on the Church, *Lumen Gentium*, 62: AAS 57 (1965), p. 63.

51. Second Vatican Council, Constitution on the Sacred Liturgy, *Sacrosanctum Concilium*, 83: AAS 56 (1964), p. 121.

52. Second Vatican Council, Dogmatic Constitution on the Church, *Lumen Gentium*, 63: AAS 57 (1965), p. 64.

53. *Ibid.*, 64: AAS 57 (1965), p. 64.

54. *Tractatus XXV (In Nativitate Domini)*, 5: *CCL* 138, p. 123; *S.Ch.* 22 bis, p. 132; cf. also *Tractatus XXIX (In Nativitate Domini)* 1. *CCL ibid.*, p. 147; *S. Ch. ibid.*, p. 178; *Tractatus LXIII (De Passione Domini)* 6: *CCL ibid.*, p. 386; *S.Ch.* 74, p. 82.

55. M. Ferotin, *Le Liber Mozarabicus Sacramentorum*," col. 56.

56. *In Purificatione B. Mariae. Sermo III*, 2: *PL* 183, 370; *Sancti Bernardi Opera*, ed. J. Leclercq-H. Rochais, vol. IV, Rome 1966, p. 342.

57. Cf. Second Vatican Council, Dogmatic Constitution on the Church, *Lumen Gentium*, 57: AAS 57 (1965), p. 61.

58. *Ibid.*, 58: AAS 57 (1965), p. 61.

59. Cf. Pius XII, Encyclical Letter *Mystici Corporis*: AAS 35 (1943), p. 247.

60. Cf. Second Vatican Council, Constitution on the Sacred Liturgy, *Sacrosanctum Concilium*, 47: AAS 56 (1964), p. 113.

61. *Ibid.*, 102, 106: AAS 56 (1964), pp. 125, 126.

62. "...deign to remember all who have been pleasing to you throughout the ages, the holy Fathers, the Patriarchs, Prophets, Apostles...and the holy and glorious Mother of God and all the saints...may they remember our misery and poverty, and together with us may they offer you this great and unbloody sacrifice": *Anaphora Iacobi fratris Domini syriaca: Prex Eucharistica*, ed. A. Hänggi-I. Pahl, Fribourg, *Editions Universitaires*, 1968, p. 274.

63. *Expositio Evangelii secundum Lucam*, 11, 26: *CSEL* 32, IV, p. 55; *S. Ch.* 45, pp. 83-84.

64. Cf. Second Vatican Council, Dogmatic Constitution on the Church, *Lumen Gentium*, 62: *AAS* 57 (1965), p. 63.

65. Second Vatican Council, Constitution on the Sacred Liturgy, *Sacrosanctum Concilium*, 103: *AAS* 56 (1964), p. 125.

66. Second Vatican Council, Dogmatic Constitution on the Church, *Lumen Gentium*, 67: *AAS* 57 (1965), pp. 65-66.

67. Cf. *Ibid.*

68. Cf. Second Vatican Council, Constitution on the Sacred Liturgy, *Sacrosanctum Concilium*, 104: *AAS* 56 (1964), pp. 125-126.

69. Cf. Second Vatican Council, Dogmatic Constitution on the Church, *Lumen Gentium*, 66: *AAS* 57 (1965), p. 65.

70. Cf. Paul VI, Talk of April 24, 1970, in the church of Our Lady of Bonaria in Cagliari: *AAS* 62 (1970), p. 300.

71. Pius IX, Apostolic Letter *Ineffabilis Deus: Pii IX Pontificis Maximi Acta*, I, 1, Rome 1854, p. 599. Cf. also V. Sardi, *La solenne definizione del dogma dell'Immacolato concepimento di Maria Santissima. Atti e documenti...*, Rome 1904-1905, vol. II, p. 302.

72. Cf. Second Vatican Council, Dogmatic Constitution on the Church, *Lumen Gentium*, 66: *AAS* 57 (1965), p. 65.

73. S. Ildephonsus, *De virginitate perpetua sanctae Mariae*, chapter XII: *PL* 96, 108.

74. Cf. Second Vatican Council, Dogmatic Constitution on the Church, *Lumen Gentium*, 56: *AAS* 57 (1965), p. 60 and the authors mentioned in note 176 of the document.

75. Cf. St. Ambrose, *De Spiritu Sancto II*, 37-38; *CSEL* 79 pp. 100-101; Cassian, *De incarnatione Domini II*, chapter II: *CSEL* 17, pp. 247-249; St. Bede, *Homilia* I, 3: *CCL* 122, p. 18 and p. 20.

76. Cf. St. Ambrose, *De institutione virginis*, chapter XII, 79: *PL* 16 (ed. 1880), 339; *Epistula* 30, 3 and *Epistula* 42, 7: *ibid.*, 1107 and 1175; *Expositio evangelii secundum Lucam* X, 132: *S. Ch.* 52, p. 200; S. Proclus of Constantinople,

Oratio I, 1 and *Oratio* V, 3: *PG* 65, 681 and 720; St. Basil of Seleucia, *Oratio* XXXIX, 3:*PG* 85, 433; St. Andrew of Crete, *Oratio* IV: *PG* 97, 868; St. Germanus of Constantinople, *Oratio* III, 15: *PG* 98, 305.

77. Cf. St. Jerome, *Adversus Iovinianum* I, 33: *PL* 23, 267; St. Ambrose, *Epistula* 63, 33: *PL* 16 (ed. 1880), 1249; *De institutione virginis*, chapter XVII, 105: *ibid.*, 346; *De Spiritu Sancto* III, 79-80: *CSEL* 79, pp. 182-183; Sedulius, *Hymn "Asolis ortus cardine,"* verses 13-14 *CSEL* 10, p. 164; *Hymnus Acathistos*, Str. 23; ed. I. B. Pitra, *Analecta Sacra*, I, p. 261; St. Proclus of Constantinople, *Oratio* I, 3: *PG* 65, 648; *Oratio* II, 6: *ibid.*, 700; St. Basil of Seleucia, *Oratio* IV, *In Nativitatem B. Mariae: PG* 97, 868; St. John Damascene, *Oratio* IV, 10: *PG* 96, 677.

78. Cf. Severus of Antioch, *Homilia* 57; *PO* 8, pp. 357-358; Hesychius of Jerusalem, *Homilia de sancta Maria Deipara; PG* 93; 1464; Chrysippus of Jerusalem, *Oratio in sanctam Mariam Deiparam*, 2 *PO* 19, p. 338; St. Andrew of Crete, *Oratio* V: *PG* 97, 896; St. John Damascene. *Oratio* VI, 6: *PG* 96, 972.

79. *Liber Apotheosis*, verses 571-572: *CCL* 126, p. 97.

80. Cf. S. Isidore, *De ortu et obitu Patrum*, chapter LXVII 111: *PL* 83, 148; St. Ildephonsus, *De virginitate perpetua sanctae Mariae*, chapter X: *PL* 96, 95; St. Bernard, *In Assumptione B. Virginis Mariae: Sermo IV*, 4: *PL* 183, 428; *In Nativitate B. Virginis Mariae: ibid.*, 442: St. Peter Damian, *Carmina sacra et preces II, Oratio ad Deum Filium: PL* 145, 921; *Antiphon "Beata Dei Genetrix Maria": Corpus antiphonalium officii*, ed. R.J. Hesbert, Rome 1970. vol IV, n. 6314, p. 80.

81. Cf. Paulus Diaconus, *Homilia I, In Assumptione B. Mariae Virginis: PL* 95, 1567; *De Assumptione sanctae Mariae Virginis:* Paschasio Radherto trib., 31, 42, 57, 83: ed. A. Ripberger. in "Spicilegium Friburgense," 9, 1962, pp. 72, 76, 84, 96-97; Eadmer of Canterbury, *De excellentia Virginis Mariae*, chapters IV-V:*PL* 159, 562-567; St. Bernard, *In laudibus Virginis Matris, Homilia IV*, 3; *Sancti Bernardi Opera*, ed. J. Leclercq-H. Rochais, IV, Rome 1966, pp. 49-50.

82. Cf. Origen, *In Lucam Homilia* VII, 3: *PG* 13, 1817; *S. Ch.* 87, p. 156; St. Cyril of Alexandria, *Commentarius in Aggaeum prophetam*, chapter XIX:*PG* 71, 1060; St. Ambrose, *De Fide IV* 9, 113-114: *CSEL* 78, pp. 197-198; *Expositio evangelii secundum Lucam* II, 23 and 27-28: *CSEL* 32, IV, pp. 53-54 and 55-56; Severianus Gabalensis, *In mundi creationem, Oratio* VI, 10: *PG* 56 497-498; Antipater or

Bostra, *Homilia in Sanctissime Deiparae Annuntiationem,* 16: *PG* 85, 1785.

83. Cf. Eadmer of Canterbury, *De excellentia Virginis Mariae,* chapter VII: *PL* 159, 571; St. Amedeus of Lausanne, *De Maria Virgine Matre, Homilia VII: PL* 188, 1337; *S. Ch.* 72, p. 184.

84. *De Virginitate perpetua sanctae Mariae,* chapter XII: *PL* 96, 106.

85. Second Vatican Council, Dogmatic Constitution on the Church, *Lumen Gentium,* 54: *AAS* 57 (1965), p. 59. Cf. Paulus VI, *Allocutio ad Patres Conciliares habita, altera exacta Concilii Oecumenici Vaticani Secundi Sessione,* December 1963 *AAS* 56 (1964), p. 37.

86. Cf. Second Vatican Council, Dogmatic Constitution on the Church, *Lumen Gentium,* 6, 7-8, 9-11: *AAS* 57 (1965), pp. 8-9, 9-12, 12-21.

87. *Ibid.,* 63: *AAS* 57 (1965), p. 64.

88. St. Cyprian, *De Catholicae Ecclesiae unitate,* 5: *CSEL* 3, p. 214.

89. Isaac de Stella, *Sermo LI, In Assumptione B. Mariae: PL* 194, 1863.

90. *Sermo XXX,* I: *S. Ch.* 164, p. 134.

91. Cf. Second Vatican Council, Dogmatic Constitution on the Church, *Lumen Gentium,* 66-69: *AAS* 57 (1965), pp. 65-67.

92. Cf. Second Vatican Council, Dogmatic Constitution on Divine Revelation, *Dei Verbum,* 25: *AAS* 58 (1966), pp. 829-830.

93. *Op. cit.,* 13: *AAS* 56 (1964), p. 103.

94. Cf. *Officum magni canonis paracletici, Magnum Orologion,* Athens, 1963, p. 558; *passim* in liturgical canons and prayers: cf. Sophronius Eustradiadou, *Theotokarion,* Chennevières-sur Marne 1931, pp. 9, 19.

95. Cf. Second Vatican Council, Dogmatic Constitution on the Church, *Lumen Gentium,* 69: *AAS* 57 (1965), pp. 66-67.

96. Cf. *ibid.,* 66: *AAS* 57 (1965), p. 65; Constitution on the Sacred Liturgy, *Sacrosanctum Concilium,* 103: *AAS* 56 (1964), p. 125.

97. Cf. Second Vatican Council, Dogmatic Constitution on the Church, *Lumen Gentium,* 67: *AAS* 57 (1965), pp. 65-66.

98. *Ibid.,* 66: *AAS* 57 (1965), p. 65.

99. Cf. Paul VI, Address in the Vatican Basilica to the Fathers of the Council, November 21, 1964: *AAS* 56 (1964), p. 1017.

100. Second Vatican Council Decree on Ecumenism, *Unitatis Redintegratio,* 20: *AAS* 57 (1965), p. 105.

101. Encyclical Letter, *Adiutricem Populi: AAS* 28 (1895-1896), p. 135.

102. Cf. Second Vatican Council, Dogmatic Constitution on the Church, *Lumen Gentium,* 56: *AAS* 57 (1965), p. 60.

103. Cf. St. Peter Chrysologus, *Sermo CXLIII: PL* 52, 583.

104. Second Vatican Council, Dogmatic Constitution on the Church, *Lumen Gentium,* 55: *AAS* 57 (1965), pp. 59-60.

105. Cf. Paul VI, Apostolic Constitution, *Signum Magnum, I: AAS* 59 (1967), pp. 467-468; Roman Missal, September 15, Prayer over the gifts.

106. Cf. Dogmatic Constitution on the Church, *Lumen Gentium,* 67: *AAS* 57 (1965), pp. 65-66.

107. St. Augustine, *In Johannis Evangelium, Tractatus X,* 3: *CCL* 36, pp. 101-102; *Epistula* 243, *Ad Laetum,* 9: *CSEL* 57, pp. 575-576, St. Bede, *In Lucae Evangelium expositio, IV,* XI, 28: *CCL* 120, p. 237; *Homilia I,* 4: *CCL* 122, pp. 26-27.

108. Cf. Second Vatican Council, Dogmatic Constitution on the Church, *Lumen Gentium,* 58: *AAS* 57 (1965), p. 61.

109. Roman Missal, IV Sunday of Advent, Collect. Similarly the Collect of March 25, which may be used in place of the previous one in the recitation of the Angelus.

110. Pius XII, Letter to the Archbishop of Manila, *"Philippinas Insulas": AAS* 38 (1946), p. 419.

111. Discourse to the participants in the III Dominican International Rosary Congress: *Insegnamenti di Paolo VI,* 1 (1963), pp. 463-464.

112. In *AAS* 58 (1966), pp. 745-749.

113. In *AAS* 61 (1969), pp. 649-654.

114. Cf. 13: *AAS* 56 (1964), p. 103.

115. Decree on the Lay Apostolate, *Apostolicam Actuositatem,* 11: *AAS* 58 (1966), p. 848.

116. Cf. Second Vatican Council, Dogmatic Constitution on the Church, *Lumen Gentium,* 11: *AAS* 57 (1965), p. 16.

117. Cf. Second Vatican Council, Decree on the Lay Apostolate, *Apostolicam Actuositatem,* 11: *AAS* 58 (1966), p. 848.

118. *Op. Cit.,* 27.

119. Second Vatican Council, Dogmatic Constitution on the Church, *Lumen Gentium,* 53: *AAS* 57 (1965), pp. 58-59.

120. *La Divina Commedia, Paradiso XXXIII,* 4-6.

121. Cf. Second Vatican Council, Dogmatic Constitution on the Church, *Lumen Gentium*, 60-63: *AAS* 57 (1965), pp. 62-64.

122. Cf. *ibid.*, 65: *AAS* 57 (1965), pp. 64-65.

123. *Ibid.*, 65: *AAS* 57 (1965), p. 64.

124. Cf. Second Vatican Council, Pastoral Constitution on the Church in the Modern World, *Gaudium et spes*, 22: *AAS* 58 (1966), pp. 1042-1044.

125. Cf. Roman Missal, May 31, Collect.

Seeking Mary's Help
for Serious Problems Today

This was the program that became a habit of pious persons and devout communities, always left to the free initiative of the religious spirit of the faithful people. In our recent Apostolic Exhortation for the right-ordering and development of devotion to the Blessed Virgin (on last February 2), we endeavored to recall devotion to Christ's Mother to its biblical and theological foundations, and to its liturgical, official norms for the whole Church. For it is very important to have true and clear ideas, and authentic and noble expressions with regard to this extremely important part of our religious life, completely centered, as is known, on the mystery of Christ.

Yet again we affirmed the pastoral value of devotion to Mary most holy, and recalled that she has a very special mission in the divine plan of salvation, which obliges us to venerate her and imitate her, and authorizes us to place our particular trust in her motherly intercession.

Yes, Mary acts on our behalf in her heavenly bliss, through her prevailing charity in the communion of saints; she knows and listens to our invocations.

This trust now opens before us the panorama of the world, where scenes of most urgent interest inspire our prayer to the Mother of Christ, to the Mother of the Church, to the Queen of peace, to the help of Christians, to the consoler of the afflicted, to the inspirer of heavenly wisdom.

And now we invite you, too, beloved sons, to join in chorus with us in asking for her loving intervention with Jesus the Savior, let us say for example, for the holy places, beloved by us all, and for the whole of the Middle East, where we hope it will be possible in these days to settle the grave and complicated conflicts. Then we will invoke the Madonna, who has a privileged sanctuary at Lourdes, for today's elections in France; we will invoke the Madonna of Fatima for the solution of the problems in Portugal; the Madonna honored at St. Mary Major, in the sanctuaries of Oropa, Loreto and Pompei for religious peace in Italy; the Madonna of Czestochowa for Catholic Poland, which in these days is holding special celebrations there in honor of holy Mary; the Madonna invoked at Guadalupe, or at Aparicida or at Washington for the real well-being of the countries that pride themselves on these Marian sanctuaries; and then for all the countries which, in their own sanctuaries dedicated to the Virgin, invoke her protection, follow her example, profess her faith, and discover those aspects of it that give the Marian cult an incomparable incentive for the defense of woman today, in her inviolable dignity and in her modern spiritual and social vocation.

So let us say together: *Regina caeli laetare, alleluia!*

—*"Regina caeli" message, May 5, 1974 (OR)*

Strengthening Devotion to Mary in Our Time

It is true that the Sunday liturgy takes precedence over the feast of September 8, which would draw our affectionate devotion to the Nativity of the Blessed Virgin, celebrated by the traditional piety of the Church on this date. Without prejudice to the liturgical norm, we will devote this moment of private religious interest to the feast of the Blessed Virgin recalling her entrance into earthly life and upon the stage of time, and, Mother of Christ and ours as she is, her appearance as a child at the beginning of the great story of our salvation.

We have personal reasons, not unworthy of being confided to you today. We recall that the church of St. Mary of the Graces at Brescia, a few steps from our home, which we attended with daily assiduity in our youth, is dedicated to the birth of our Lady. Every year, on this feast, the Blessed Virgin had our whole family gathered punctiliously around her. Nor can we forget the lapidary dedication on the front of the ever beloved and glorious Cathedral of Milan: "Mariae Nascenti," to Mary in her birth; and the famous Madonnina that soars triumphantly aloft on the highest spire of the delightful building. And then what Roman, by birth or adoption, has not been in some way a client of the new church, the Vallicella of St. Philip Neri, which is also dedicated to the Nativity of Our Lady? These cherished memories of ours tell you that we, like the whole Church, willingly see in this Marian festivity "the hope and the dawn of salvation for the whole world" (Roman Missal, September 8, postcomm.); and now we are taking this opportunity to revive in you, too, a new and warm-hearted devotion to Mary.

You certainly know that on last February 2 we addressed to all the bishops, and therefore to the whole Church, a special exhortation "For the right ordering and development of devotion to the Blessed Virgin Mary." We recommend everyone to read it!

Let not this sweet and motherly light of devotion to our Lady be weakened, or extinguished in our modern generation. Today, with the memory of her birth, this light is kindled again on earth for the better destiny of mankind. But may it shine forth more than ever to enkindle in our hearts faith and love of Christ, and to teach each of us with what fortitude this blessed among women replied: Yes! to God's plans of salvation for the world.

—*Angelus message, September 8, 1974 (OR)*

Marian Cult: an Important, Dynamic Aspect of the Religious Spirit

Venerable brothers in the Episcopate and beloved sons of Chile,

We address you joyfully on such a special and solemn occasion as is the consecration of the national votive temple, dedicated to Our Lady of Carmel, at Maipù.

We are exceedingly pleased to know that, responding promptly to the initiative of your Episcopate, the Chilean Catholic community has vibrated spontaneously and unanimously to the appeal to pay deep and loving homage, as the best culmination of the Holy Year, to the heavenly Patroness of Chile, so closely linked to the history and life of your people.

Marian devotion, in fact, which flowered so soon in Aimarà and Quichua culture, has grown deeper and deeper roots among you, constituting an important and dynamic aspect of your religious spirit and helping it to find concrete expression in the realities of every moment. It is as if ancient and recent history—a past full of achievement and a present eager to project, with redoubled desire for spiritual and human progress, the legitimate aspirations of all to an environment increasingly united in Christian solidarity and brotherly participation —had found genuine expression around the mystery of Mary.

We wish today to exhort you to continue along this path, perfecting it more and more. Mary is, in fact, the model par excellence of the Church; an always valid model of faith, as response to God's word, the premise and spring of her marvellous divine motherhood; the model of operating love, of active and inspiring presence in the prayerful community of the apostles (cf. Apostolic Exhortation on the Cult of the Blessed Virgin, nn. 16-21), who "shines forth on earth, until the day of the Lord shall come, as a sign of sure hope and solace for the pilgrim People of God" (*Lumen Gentium,* 68).

So we can declare ourselves fortunate to have the Mother of Jesus as Mother in the Church. Associated mysteriously and for ever with the work of Christ, she "continues to win for us gifts of eternal salvation" (*ibid.,* 62). This constant concern of hers for the elect (cf. *ibid.*) cannot but be a real inner incentive in the hearts of all her sons, beating in harmony, to discover in every fellow being a brother "sealed with the promised Holy Spirit, who is the guarantee of our inheritance until we acquire possession of it..." (Eph. 1:14). And it is in full, heartfelt adherence to this patrimony of the Spirit that the aspirations to renewal and reconciliation, individual and social, which constitute the aims of the Holy Year, must find their point of convergence and stimulation.

Real devotion to Mary will therefore bring as a natural fruit for you, Chileans, and for all those who on this memorable date participate in your Marian fervor, an increasing commitment of service to the Gospel, with a genuine effort to bring to all men the message of salvation and to construct the kingdom of God in solidarity among those liberated by Christ. In this way, "while honoring Christ's Mother, these devotions cause her Son to be rightly known, loved, and glorified" (cf. *Lumen Gentium*, 66).

We hope and trust that you, beloved sons of Chile, nourishing in your spirit an ever rejuvenated communion in the ideals of Christian progress, will succeed in opening the way to a new ecclesial blossoming, established on love, in the life of that beloved country. We lay these wishes of ours before Our Lady of Carmel at Maipù, to whom we have also wished to pay homage with the donation of a cape and a crown, symbols of filial trust in her powerful protection. Invoking her precious intercession with the Lord so that He will always assist the beloved sons of this nation and reward all those whose efforts made possible this beautiful National Shrine, we bless you all in the name of the Father, the Son and the Holy Spirit.

— Message to the bishops and people of Chile,
November 24, 1974 (OR)

Mary Immaculate,
the Image of Perfection

The Immaculate: this feast of our Lady arouses within us a warm enthusiasm, which in a certain sense hides the depth of the mystery; the mystery of original sin, the universal misfortune inherited by mankind from their father Adam. This misfortune separated us from God, produced a functional disorder in our being that not even baptism cures completely, restored death to our natural life. It has left deep down in our inextinguishable aspirations a wistful longing for a perfection that we are no longer able to reach, not even the best of us, the good, the great, the wise and the very saints themselves. We are unhappy, we are a fallen race: the mystery of the devastation that has spread over humankind.

But today we are seized with a great wonder, a great joy: one creature, one only, but ours, she that was to be the Mother of Christ, was redeemed in advance by Christ Himself and restored to the original perfection, typical and sublime, of the creature "full of grace," a woman, "blessed among all women." Her name is Mary.

Sons and brothers, disappointed perhaps and despairing at the discovery by modern psychoanalytical researches of the incurable contamination of the depths of the human being, renew with confidence the concept of innocence and the hope of the perfect purity of this being of ours composed of flesh and spirit: the "case," the miracle, of Mary rehabilitates in us the image of the perfection of the work of God, which we are, and of which an intact and absolutely pure model is presented to us: yes, it is Mary.

You who are in search of beauty, who, too often seeking it in the imbalance between flesh and spirit, deface it, remember that purity and beauty coincide: "by antonomasia beauty is attributed to chastity – Thomas Aquinas teaches – and therefore virginity is most excellently beautiful" (S. Theol. II, II, 152, 4). And so today we sing with the Church: you are all beautiful, oh Mary!

Are you seeking the joy and liberation of a new life? Recite the "Magnificat," pondering it as you do so; it is the prophetic hymn of the Immaculate.

So love, real love: it is the Holy Spirit, divine charity, of which Mary was the radiant treasury; let us seek it in her, with her.

It is a happy day, therefore, the feast of the Immaculate. Suffocated as we might appear to be by the degrading licentiousness of rampant vice and pornography, let us defend ourselves by enjoying a feast such as today's, which is all purity, all beauty, all love! Today the Immaculate Madonna is with us. Shall we meet again this afternoon in the Piazza di Spagna?

—*Angelus message, December 8, 1974 (OR)*

Reawakening
Devotion to Mary

Venerable brothers and dear sons and daughters,

Having been present in thought, by our prayers and with our paternal exhortation at the activities of your Mariological Congress, it has seemed to us as it were a duty deriving from our awareness of being universal Pastor of the Church to take part also by our presence in this closing meeting. And by prolonging in a certain way with our thought this visit of ours, we wish to extend our greetings both to you and also to all those who will be taking part in the fourteenth Marian Congress.

We are moved to do so above all by our love for the Blessed Virgin Mary, Mother of God and of the Church, as well as of each of us. Assuring us that Mary is the Mother of God (cf. Lk. 1:26ff.), the Gospel offers us also the solid basis — that no shadow of doubt can touch — for rendering to Mary the honor due to her and the outpouring of affection which like a gentle echo redounds to her Son.

We have also been moved by the consideration of the importance which this Congress assumes in the climate and context of the Holy Year. If indeed the Blessed Virgin is the one "full of grace" (Lk. 1:28) who has given us Jesus Christ, then everyone can see how her example, her intercession, and her protection can help the faithful to renew themselves and to be reconciled with God and with their brethren, in the absence and avoidance of all sin.

We likewise wished to render due homage to those who have promoted these two Congresses and to thank them, because their example of filial love to the Mother of Christ and their deep studies of the person and the mission of Mary cannot but prove very fruitful for the Church. We are therefore grateful in the first place to our very dear Cardinal Leo Jozef Suenens, President of the Congresses; to Father Carlo Balic, O.F.M., President of the Pontifical International Marian Academy; to the Rector Magnificus of this Pontifical Athenaeum Antonianum, Father Roberto Zavalloni; together with the illustrious speakers, the Marian Associations which have lent their support, and all the numerous participants. We would express the wish that for all there may be verified the words spoken of wisdom and applied by the Church to the Blessed Virgin: *Qui elucidant me, vitam aeternam habebunt* (Sir. 24:31).

Moreover, the themes chosen by these two Congresses merit particular consideration

and praise on our part: the first one, the Mariological Congress, is concerned with devotion
to the Blessed Virgin from the twelfth to the
fifteenth centuries; the other, the Marian Congress, is concerned with the Holy Spirit and the
Blessed Virgin. It would be difficult to think of
more opportune and interesting themes.

Above all we are pleased to note that the two
Congresses have very happily been inserted
into the context of present theological research
and the new dimension of Marian piety, as
authoritatively outlined by the teaching of the
Second Vatican Council: a teaching which has
placed in right perspective the place that belongs
to the Blessed Virgin in the mystery of Christ
and of the Church and which now constitutes
a masterpiece which a true development of
Mariology and a healthy orientation of the faithful towards the Mother of God and our Mother
cannot ignore.

From the fact that "when the appointed time
came, God sent his Son, born of a woman"
(Gal. 4:4), and Mary, as the Council teaches,
"was not a purely passive instrument in the
hands of God, but cooperated in the salvation
of mankind by her free faith and obedience"
(*Lumen Gentium*, 56), it follows that Mary
assumes an essential part in the mystery of
salvation.

Christ has come to us through Mary; we
have received Him from her. If therefore we
want to be true Christians we must recognize
the essential and vital relationship which
united the Blessed Virgin to Jesus and which

opens for us the way that leads to Him. We cannot detach our gaze from her who, as the Council teaches, is the creature most like Christ, the "type" of the Church and "the most excellent model of faith and love" (*Lumen Gentium*, 53; cf. 61, 65).

This teaching must always be kept in mind, because it is the foundation of that relationship of love, honor and veneration which we owe to Mary and which rightly and most felicitously goes under the name of Marian devotion—provided it keeps the meaning which the Church has given it. We have already recalled this in our Apostolic Exhortation *Marialis Cultus:* "...in the expressions of devotion to the Virgin the Christological aspect should have particular prominence. It likewise seems to us fitting that these expressions of devotion should reflect God's plan, which laid down 'with one single decree the origin of Mary and the Incarnation of the divine wisdom.'" This fact will without doubt not only not diminish but "will also contribute to increasing the worship due to Christ Himself, since, according to the perennial mind of the Church... 'what is given to the handmaid is referred to the Lord; thus what is given to the Mother redounds to the Son; ...and thus what is given as humble tribute to the Queen becomes honor rendered to the King'" (*Marialis Cultus*, 25).

In this way "devotion to the Mother of the Lord becomes for the faithful an opportunity for growing in divine grace and this is the ultimate aim of all pastoral activity. For it is impossible to honor her who is 'full of grace' (Lk. 1:28) without thereby honoring in oneself the state of grace, which is friendship with God, communion with Him and the indwelling of the Holy Spirit. It is this divine grace which takes possession of the whole man and conforms him to the image of the Son of God..." *(Marialis Cultus,* 57).

From what we have said so far, you can easily understand the great importance which we attribute to the two Congresses now being celebrated. They will surely be a seed which will bring forth abundant and salutary fruits not only in the Mariological field but also in the theological, liturgical, ecumenical and above all the pastoral field. Indeed, continuing in this way the work undertaken by the two previous Congresses organized by the Pontifical International Marian Academy, on the one hand there are compared the researches on one of the most fruitful periods in the affirmation and promotion of Marian devotion, by the initiatives above all of theologians like St. Albert the Great, St. Thomas, John Duns Scotus, St. Bonaventure, to mention just some of the most illustrious names which strove to study more deeply the mission and prerogatives of the Blessed Virgin. And on the other hand the study of the relationship between the Holy Spirit and Mary which constitutes the specific objective of the Marian Congress can offer a clear contribution concerning the role of each in the plan of salvation. In this regard, we stated in the Apostolic Exhortation already mentioned:

"It is sometimes said that many spiritual writings today do not sufficiently reflect the whole doctrine concerning the Holy Spirit" (*Marialis Cultus*, 27). And we added: "It is the task of specialists to verify and weigh the truth of this assertion..." (*ibid.*). We therefore consider your two Congresses as the most qualified forum to respond to these expectations.

We could conclude our considerations at this point, were it not that we are urged by the nobility of this theme to add a flower to the contribution of teaching which, like a precious crown, you intend in this Holy Year to place at the feet of the Blessed Virgin. It is a flower that we like to gather more from our heart than from our reflection, in view of a pastoral rather than a scientific purpose—though the latter is likewise present in the homage which these Congresses (the first Congress not excluded) wish to offer to Mary. We would like to respond to a question of great pastoral and also doctrinal relevance: how to represent Mary in an adequate way to the People of God in such a way as to reawaken in them the fervor of renewed Marian piety?

PATH OF FAITH

In this there are two paths that can be followed. The path of truth, first of all—that is, biblical, historical and theological speculation—which concerns Mary's exact place in the mystery of Christ and the Church. This is the path of the learned, the one which you are following; it is certainly necessary and from it

Mariological teaching derives advantage. But there is also, besides this one, a path accessible to all, including the least educated. It is the path of beauty, to which the mysterious, marvelous and stupendous teaching which forms the theme of the Marian Congress finally leads us: Mary and the Holy Spirit. In fact, Mary is the creature "all beautiful"; she is the mirror without spot, and the supreme ideal of perfection which the artists of every period have endeavored to reproduce in their works. She is the "woman clothed with the sun" (Rv. 12:1), in whom the purest rays of human beauty mingle with those sovereign inaccessible rays of supernatural beauty. And what is the reason for all this? Because Mary is the one "full of grace," that is, we can say, full of the Holy Spirit, whose light shone forth in her with incomparable splendor. Yes, we need to look to Mary, to fix our gaze on her unsullied beauty, for our eyes are too often offended and almost blinded by the deceiving images of beauty in this world. How many noble sentiments, how great a desire for purity, what renewing spirituality can be evoked by the contemplation of such sublime beauty.

MARY'S EXAMPLE

While, in our day, woman is advancing in the life of society, there is nothing more beneficial or elevating than the example of this Virgin Mother, radiant with the Holy Spirit, who with her beauty sums up and incarnates the true values of the human spirit.

Let us therefore strive, venerable brothers and dear sons and daughters, to ensure that in our modern generation the kindly and maternal light of devotion to Mary does not grow dim but is ever more strongly rekindled. And with these hopes we cordially impart to all of you here present and to all the participants in the Congresses, in pledge of divine graces, our apostolic blessing.

—Address to the participants of the International Mariological and Marian Congresses, May 16, 1975 (OR)

May Devotion to the Blessed Virgin Mary Shine Forth in All Hearts

To our Venerable Brother Cardinal Leo Jozef Suenens, Archbishop of Mechelen-Brussels:

It is with sentiments of great confidence and deep joy that we greet the participants in the International Marian Congress, sponsored and organized by the well-deserving International Pontifical Academy. Its subject, in fact, not only fits admirably into the context of the celebrations of the Jubilee Year, but seems to confer on them a new incomparable fascination.

There is no doubt, in fact, that the Holy Year calls for interior purification and the progress of spirits on the way to holiness. But how could we fail to hope that examination and study of the interior ties, pure and sacred, that bound and still bind the Virgin Mary to the Holy Spirit in the work of human redemption, will yield extremely useful results, not only for the development of Catholic dogma and theological science, but also for increase of the worship of the Holy Spirit and the cult of the Mother of God and Mother of the Church?

We are aware that Catholic theology has insisted more, in our times, on study of the Marian truths, preserved in the Holy Scripture and in divine Tradition, in order to explain their content and shed light on their salutary effects. But this praiseworthy intention, crowned by abundant fruit, has not dimmed the primacy of faith and worship that the whole Church bestows on the Holy Spirit, in conformity with the Creed "Quicumque"; "Patris et Filii et Spiritus Sancti una est divinitas, aequalis gloria, coaeterna maiestas" (PL 88, 585 s). This holds good above all for liturgical worship, which is the genuine and best known expression of faith and Christian piety, according to the well-known axiom: "Lex orandi, lex credendi" (Pius XII, Enc. Mediator Dei: A.A.S. 39, 1947, p. 541).

RECOGNITION OF MARY'S STATUS

The Catholic Church, moreover, has always believed that the Holy Spirit, intervening personally, even though in indivisible communion with the other Persons of the Holy Trinity, in the work of human salvation (cf. G. Philips, L'Union personelle avec le Dieu vivant. Essai sur l'origine et le sens de la grâce créé, 1974), has associated the humble virgin of Nazareth with Himself. So the Church has

thought that He has done so in a way in keeping
with His nature as personal love of the Father
and the Son, that is, with an action at once very
powerful and very sweet, so as to adapt perfectly the person of Mary, with all her faculties
and energies both spiritual and physical, to the
tasks reserved for her on the plane of redemption
(cf. St. Thomas, *Sum. Theol.* III, q. 27). On
the basis of this belief, which springs from the
increasingly deep and clear understanding
of the sacred texts, Fathers and Doctors of the
Church, both in the East and in the West, have
attributed to the various missions of the Holy
Spirit, proceeding from the Father and from
the Son, the fullness of grace and charity of
the gifts and fruits of every virtue, as well as
of the evangelical beatitudes and special charisms, which adorned, like a trousseau for a
heavenly wedding, the predestined mystical
bride of the divine Paraclete and Mother of
the Word of God, become flesh. It is, in fact,
because of her privileges and exceptional
gifts of grace, all coming from the divine Spirit,
that Mary is greeted in the Sacred Liturgy:
"Templum Domini, sacrarium Spiritus Sancti."

MARY, FULL OF GRACE

It will, therefore, be a source of great
comfort for us to dwell in joyful contemplation
of the principal operations of the Spirit of
Christ on the elect Mother of God. It was the
Holy Spirit who, filling with grace the person

of Mary at the first moment of her conception, redeemed her in a more sublime way in view of the merits of Christ the Savior of mankind and therefore made her Immaculate (cf. Pius IX, *Bull Ineffabilis Deus*, December 8, 1854; DS. 2803); it was the Holy Spirit who, coming upon her, inspired her to agree, on behalf of mankind, to the virginal conception of God's Son and fertilized her womb so that she might give birth to the Savior of her people, the sovereign of an everlasting kingdom (cf. Lk. 1:35-38). Again, it was the Holy Spirit that inflamed her spirit with joy and gratitude, thus stimulating her to burst into the *Magnificat* in praise of God, her Savior (cf. Lk. 1:45-55); it was likewise the Holy Spirit that gave the Virgin the good advice to keep faithfully in her heart the memory of the words and facts concerning the birth and childhood of her only Son, in which she had taken such a close and loving part (cf. Lk. 2:19; 33:51). Yet again, it was the Holy Spirit that induced Mary to request from her Son the miracle of the transformation of the water into wine at the Cana wedding, the first of His miracles, thus bringing about the faith of His disciples (cf. Jn. 2:11). It was the Holy Spirit that sustained the Mother of Jesus, present at the foot of His cross, inspiring her, as already in the Annunciation, with the *Fiat* to the will of the heavenly Father, who wished her to be maternally associated with the sacrifice of her Son for the redemption of mankind (cf. Jn. 19:25). It was the Holy

Spirit that enlarged, with immense charity, the
heart of the grieving Mother, so that she would
accept from the lips of her Son, as His last testament, the mission of Mother to His beloved disciple John (cf. Jn. 19:26-27), foreshadowing,
"according to the perennial sense of the Church"
(Leo XIII, Enc. *Adiutricem populi:* September 5, 1895: *Acta Leonis* XIII, vol. XV, p. 302)
her spiritual motherhood for the benefit of
the whole of mankind. Again, it was the Holy
Spirit that raised Mary, on the wings of the
most fervent charity, to her role of prayer in
the upper room, where Jesus' disciples "gave
themselves up to prayer, together with Mary
the Mother of Jesus, and the rest of the women"
(Acts 1:14), in expectation of the promised
Paraclete. Finally, it was the Holy Spirit that,
burning with supreme ardor in the heart of
Mary, a pilgrim on earth, made her very eager
to join her glorious Son and so prepared her
to attain in a worthy way, as the crowning
point of her privileges, her assumption in soul
and body into heaven, according to the dogmatic definition (cf. Pius XII, Apost. Const.
Munificentissimus Deus, November 1, 1950,
AAS, 42, 1950, p. 768), the XXV anniversary
of which, as we recall with particular emotion,
falls this year.

But Mary's mission as partner of the Spirit
of Christ in the mystery of salvation, did not end
with her glorious assumption. Although absorbed in joyful contemplation of the blessed
Trinity, she continues to be present spiritually
to all the redeemed, always stimulated to her

noble office by divine Love, the soul of the
Mystical Body and its supreme Mover.

Mary's incessant presence within the pilgrim Church was confirmed by the Second Vatican Council, which declared: "This maternity
of Mary in the order of grace...will last without
interruption.... For, taken up to heaven, she
did not lay aside this saving role, but by her
manifold acts of intercession continues to win
for us gifts of eternal salvation" (*Lumen Gentium*, 62).

BY ALL GENERATIONS

It is, therefore, a worthy and just thing that
the Holy Mother of God, as she has been called
since the early centuries of the Church (An-
tiph. *Sub tuum praesidium),* should continue to
be "called blessed by all generations" *(Magnificat)* and to be "invoked by the Church under
the titles of *Advocate, Auxiliatrix, Adjutrix*
and *Mediatrix*" *(Lumen Gentium,* 62); but,
as the Council wisely admonishes: "these,
however, are to be so understood that they
neither take away from nor add anything to the
dignity and efficacy of Christ the one Mediator"
(ibid.); and, we must add, in such a way that
they do not take away anything from the dignity
and efficacy of the Spirit, who is the Sanctifier
both of the Head and of the individual members
of the Mystical Body.

We must consider, therefore, that the
action of the Mother of the Church, for the
benefit of the redeemed, does not replace, or

compete with, the almighty and universal action of the Holy Spirit, but implores and prepares it, not only with *prayer* of intercession, in harmony with the divine plans contemplated in the beatific vision, but also with the direct influence of *example,* including, what is extremely important, maximum docility to the inspirations of the divine Spirit (cf. Dogm. Const. *Lumen Gentium,* 63-65). It is, therefore, always dependent on the Holy Spirit that Mary leads souls to Jesus, forms them in her image, inspires them with good advice and is a tie of love between Jesus and believers.

ANCIENT TESTIMONY

In confirmation of these reflections, we are happy to recall the testimony that also the Fathers and Doctors of the Eastern Church, exemplary as they are in the faith and in worship of the Holy Spirit, have borne to ecclesial faith and the cult of the Mother of Christ, as the mediator of divine favors. Their affirmations, however surprising, should not disturb anyone, since it is understood and sometimes clearly mentioned in them that the source of the Virgin's mediating action is dependent on the action of the Spirit of God. So, for example, St. Ephraem exalts Mary in these superlative tones: "Blessed is she who has been made the source for the whole world, emanating all goods" (*S. Ephraem Syri hymni et serm.,* ed. Th. Lamy Malines, 1882-1902, II, p. 548); and again: "Most holy Lady...; the only one that has been made the dwelling of all the graces of the Holy Spirit"

(*Assem. graec. III*, 542). St. John Chrysostom sums up Mary's salvific work in the following stupendous eulogy: "A virgin chased us out of paradise; thanks to the intervention of another virgin, we have found eternal life again. As we were condemned by the fault of a virgin, so we have been crowned by the merit of a virgin" (*Expos. in ps.* 44, 7: *PG* 55, 193). They are echoed, in the eighth century, by St. Germanus of Constantinople, who addresses the following moving invocations to Mary: "You, oh pure, excellent and most merciful Lady, comfort of Christians..., protect us with the wings of your kindness; guard us with your intercession, giving us eternal life; you who are the hope of Christians that does not deceive...Your gifts are innumerable. For no one, unless through you, oh holy one, obtains salvation. No one, unless through you, is delivered from evil. Who like you, in agreement with your only Son, looks after mankind?" (*Concio in sanctam Mariam: PG* 98, 327).

AN INCOMPARABLE MODEL

This traditional faith, which is common both to the Eastern and to the Western Church, found authoritative confirmation in the teaching of our great predecessor Leo XIII, who, while he published numerous encyclical letters to promote the cult of the Mother of God, invoked especially under the title of Queen of the Holy Rosary, also dedicated a long and documented encyclical to the exaltation, even more excellent, of the Holy Spirit and promotion

of His worship (Enc. *Divinum illud munus,*
May 9, 1897; *Acta Leonis XIII,* Vol. XVII, pp.
126-148).

In this particularly critical hour for the
history of the Church and the fate of humanity,
in which the interior renewal of Christians
and their reconciliation with God and among
themselves are indispensable requisites for the
Church to be in Christ "a kind of sacrament
or sign of intimate union with God, and of the
unity of all mankind" *(Lumen Gentium,* 1),
the worship of the Spirit, the sovereign source
of charity, unity and peace, must excel in the soul
of the faithful; but, in harmony with it, kindled
and enlivened by the fire of divine Love, the
cult of the great Mother of God, Mother of the
Church, the incomparable model of love of God
and of our brothers, must also shine in the hearts
of the faithful.

Recommending our considerations to the
loving reflection of the participants in the
International Marian Congress, we express the
most fervent wishes for the success of the study
meetings, which will be worthily crowned by
manifestations of Christian solidarity and of
cult for the Blessed Virgin; and to you, Your
Eminence, to the zealous President of the International Pontifical Academy, to the lecturers
at the congress and to all participants, we
impart, as a sign of the particular outpouring of
the gifts of the Holy Spirit and of the motherly
protection of the Mother of God, our apostolic
blessing.

From the Vatican, May 13, 1975.

Cult of Christ and Mary Inseparable

We still retain the vivid spiritual impression created yesterday, Feast of the Assumption of Mary, by the beautiful and impressive ceremony celebrated in St. Peter's in honor of the Madonna. Her venerated image, known as "Salus Populi Romani," was carried in procession from St. Mary Major as part of the Holy Year ceremonies, so that the overflow crowd of pilgrims, coming from all parts of the world, could see it and thus increase their devotion to her. In this way we should all be reminded of the meaning and the practice of the cult of Mary, inseparable from the unique and central cult of Christ.

We have seen the People of God joyfully absorbed in the contemplation and invocation of Mary. They want to be assured that Mary, already assumed body and soul into heaven, is not on that account further away from us, but rather, for that very reason, closer to us. I want to repeat this to you — why closer?

We would like to see a much more wide-spread knowledge of the teaching that was drawn up by the Council about Mary. It is to be found in Chapter VIII, the concluding chapter of the fundamental Constitution *Lumen Gentium*, that great synthesis of teaching on the Church, and consequently on her who is the "typical example" of the Church, spiritually a universal Mother, ideal and beloved. We could also suggest for your devotion, the reading of our apostolic exhortation, of February last year, on "The Cult of Mary." We trust that this would result in positive thought for ecclesial communion.

From a better understanding of the unique and most apt place assigned to Mary in the religious plan for our salvation, a position that no other can take or suppress, it must needs be that a feeling springs up which brings strength and comfort to all. This feeling is one of a great trust in the intercession of Mary, who knows our needs, who listens to our prayers, who helps us along the wearisome road towards the victorious goal of eternal life "now and at the hour of our death."

There is no need to say that this will result in a vindication, a strengthening, a sublimation of our modern feminism. This year we are celebrating throughout the world Woman's Year, to which the Church, as in duty bound, gives her full support. She gladly looks forward to an advance in the contribution made by woman in professional and social life. She likewise protects the dignity and the mission of woman, especially Christian woman, for the destiny which God has planned for her as gentle daughter, as chaste and pure maiden, as loving wife, above all, as ever-worthy and honored mother, and likewise as widow, devout, sorrowful, hard-working.

We are convinced that, in the Christian concept of woman, we ought to find recognition of her civic and human rights, and the protection of her superlative natural prerogatives. This takes place under the guiding light and protection of Mary, who, radiant in loveliness and sanctity, along with Christ, exercises her maternal sway over human destinies.

Let us together pray to her with humble, trusting and childlike love!

—Angelus message, August 17, 1975 (OR)

Necessity of
Marian Prayer

A popular and traditional devotion, but with a comtemplative and evangelical background, so often praised and recommended by our predecessors, by Pope Leo XIII especially, assigns the month of October to the cult of the Blessed Virgin, honored and invoked with the prayer of the holy rosary. Well, we are making a particular reference to it today, in order that the rosary may return among the good customs of the Christian people. Our Cardinal Vicar says so very well today in an invitation of his to the clergy and faithful of Rome. We will have present with the sick at the Holy Mass in the afternoon, in this square, also many groups who have special devotion to the rosary.

We are saying this now because we perceive an increased need for prayer. We need to pray more so that we can re-establish order in souls. Today, in modern life the attention of all of us is so divided; progress, in a certain sense, works against us; it absorbs us, it turns us outwards, it gives us the illusion of fostering the development of our personal life, while in fact it is being emptied, absorbed as it is by a growing interest in empty images and exterior occupations; we live more outside ourselves than in conversation with our conscience and with the religious realities dominating our lives and demanding filial conversation and the tribute of our speaking faith.

And then we need to pray more to obtain a greater influence of divine causality, and the assistance of the communion of saints, where Mary is Mother and Queen, in the order, or rather the disorder, of our temporal affairs, of the world. Not all of these affairs are going well. Look! Look at those phenomena that point out the inadequacies in our educational systems: where are certain young people of our times going? What is going to happen with them? Look at the economic conditions of our society: it seems to be desperate with fear of hunger and want. Look at international life: the peoples seem to be tempted to fall back upon the fatal and uncivil forms of ideological, political, military and nationalistic contests, without a common basis of human idealism and Christian love. The horizon of history is becoming dark again.

We need an active supernatural stream of wisdom and charity to flow more abundantly and mercifully in the embittered confusion of the purely natural and profane factors of human vicissitudes. Prayer wishes to be the channel of this divine, marvelous stream, which can lead to a happy end every unlucky twist of human causalities.

It is necessary to pray, to pray more, we repeat; and Mary can be the sovereign teacher and sublime partner of our stammering prayer.

—Angelus message, October 5, 1975 (OR)

Reflections on Time, the Mother of God, Peace

Venerable brothers, beloved sons!

Three subjects, three thoughts nourish our New Year's meditation today.

The first one is the thought of the civil calendar which begins with a day, not different from the others which follow one another and record the course of our present life, life in time. The fact that the numbering of the days begins again with a number one, that it inaugurates a new year and that this period of the solar cycle to which we give the name "year," resumes its punctual and inexorable revolution in solar space, makes us think of a great and undefinable cosmic and philosophical reality, which pervades our present existence: it is time! And what is time? It is the movement of a created being, it is the transient and precarious life of things that do not have in themselves the principle of their own being, and therefore do not possess immobility, eternity.

It is a continual fading away, to find oneself again in a subsequent state. "Cotidie morior" (1 Cor. 15:31), I die every day, St. Paul said. It is the precariousness of our existence, which seeks escape from its radical deficiency in motion.

GOD'S GIFT OF TIME

This is a difficult meditation, which has strained the thought of the greatest minds (cf. St. Augustine, *Confess.* XI, 24; PL, 32, 821); but which is easily expressed in the religious outlook, ours, when we remember the Lord's words: "Are there not twelve hours in the day? If any one walks in the day, he does not stumble..." (Jn. 11:9). Words in which there is the whole teaching that we must be anxious to remember: time is precious, time passes, time is a phase of experiment with regard to our decisive and definitive fate. Our future and eternal destiny depends on the proof we give of faithfulness to our duties. Time is a gift from God; it is a question posed by God's love to our free and, it can be said, fateful answer. We must be sparing of time, in order to use it well, in the intense activity of our life of work, love and suffering. Idleness or boredom have no place in the life of a Christian! Rest, yes, if necessary (cf. Mk. 6:31), but always with a view to vigilance, which only on the last day will open to a light on which the sun will never set. (On the use of time: cf. Eccl. 3:2ff.; Dan. 8:19.)

MOTHERHOOD OF MARY

Our second thought is about the festivity to which this first day of the liturgical year is dedicated, the motherhood of Mary, the Mother of God. It is, as it were, a conclusion, a crowning of the Christmas mystery. A beautiful, rich, sweet subject. There are so many things to enjoy at this first liturgical event which leads us once again along our path in that time that is still granted to us to live of this eve of eternity, which our present life is. The person of Mary, as she is presented to us in the Gospel and in Catholic worship, in her immaculate, virginal figure, in her humility and poverty, in her simplicity, is so sweet and so human, so innocent, such as we will never find in any other creature. And in the liturgy of today she is presented to us in her incomparable, ineffable and, for us, indispensable mystery, that of the Mother of Jesus Christ, the Son of God and our Savior.

Here we must make a resolution, a commitment! We will take with us, in our thought, in our devotion, in our confidence, the thought, the cult, the love of the Blessed Virgin, in every day of the year, as a "mirror," and example of every human and Christian virtue, as the pure and sweet woman who accompanies us on our tiring pilgrimage, as a Mother so great-hearted as to contain within her the fullness of love of Christ, her Son, of God the Father, the Word and the Holy Spirit, and then love of mankind, of the whole Church, of each of us. *Mater*

pulchrae dilectionis, the enlightened devotion
of the Church calls her; let us never forget.
(And let us take care to reread what chapter VIII
of the great Constitution on the Church, *Lumen
Gentium*, of the Second Vatican Ecumenical
Council, sums up for us on theology and devotion to Mary. And if you do not mind, reread
also our exhortation on Devotion to Mary, writ-
ten in February of 1974). Mary deserves this
filial interest of ours; and we have only to
draw benefit and hope from it.

THE THOUGHT OF PEACE

And the third thought cannot but be, as
you can imagine, the one that has, as every
year, brought us all here, or to various churches
in Rome, namely the thought of peace. Today
is the World Day of Peace: a day devoted to
the exaltation of peace, the admonition to
peace, reflection on the frailty and the unique
preciousness of peace.

We do not need to stress these concepts:
you know how near they are to our heart, because we have set them forth repeatedly to your
attention. We entrusted them again recently
to the message sent, for the celebration of the
Day of Peace of this year, which is just beginning, to all government leaders and rulers
of peoples, to those responsible at the various
levels of social and international life, to the
followers of the great religions, to believers,
to the faithful sons of the Church. In it we
spoke of the real arms of peace, the ones that

ensure civil society its serene stability by driving home more and more deeply in men's conscience the sense of universal brotherhood. We indicated once more the dangers, the anxieties, the sparks that can bring fatal destruction to a world that is, unfortunately, still founded on precarious balances, when not on latent or open hostilities. We described as if in a prophetic vision the forward progress of peace advancing "armed only with an olive branch" but, at the same time, being the one irreplaceable guarantee of the progress of civilization. And scrutinizing anxiously the not always encouraging symptoms of the time in which we live, we made a heartfelt appeal for peace, "armed only with goodness and love."

APPEAL TO ALL MANKIND

Today, at the dawn of the new year, we nourish the firm hope that this progress will advance with more certain firmness, at a quicker pace, encouraged on its path by larger numbers of fervent and eager supporters: Peace is possible, peace is a duty for us, peace is necessary. There is entering into the conscience of peoples the firm and decided conviction that it is impossible to construct anything effective and lasting for the good of man unless in mutual concord, in respect of reciprocal rights, in the patient experiment of constructive talks and just and sincere negotiations. And looking at what is happening on this day on which—as its joyful and ever wider echoes reach us every

year—in the capitals of the various states of
the world, at the seats of the international
organizations, in ecclesial communities, civil
and religious leaders stop for a pause of meditated reflection, nay more, of common prayer,
then deep joy fills our heart. Here we have the
real arms of peace, which is gaining ground,
though with difficulty and slowly, and pro-
gressing in the hearts of men enlightened by
God's light.

From this Chair of truth and peace, the
authentic interpreter of the message of the Son
of God, we repeat our appeal, our invitation.
To those in whose hands are the fates of peoples, or rather the life or death of millions of
brothers, we repeat our passionate exhortation:
the innocent and imploring eyes of children
of the poor, of those suffering in body or in
spirit from the wounds of war, beseech them,
the judgment of history is lying in wait for them,
but, more severe and infallible, God's judgment awaits them. Let no effort be left untried
to settle disagreements, overcome difficulties
and promote human and social progress, especially where need is greatest and difficulties
most pressing.

But we address individuals, too: you who are
listening to us in this devout and luminous
gathering, those who are connected with us
by radio, the persons who form the connective
tissue of society, the "man in the street." We
are all responsible for peace, we are all called
to collaborate for peace, making our personal
contribution to the building-up of a society

based on love, in our environment, our profession, and daily relations. We are all called to fight with the powerful arms of love and brotherhood for the establishment, safeguarding and diffusion of peace around us. Let each one begin by himself; the number will grow enormously; it is a work to which no one must remain extraneous.

We entrust these ardent wishes to the wisdom and goodness of Him who is the Prince of Peace. May He strengthen good dispositions with His grace. And we also entrust our hopes to her who, showing Him to the world as the Author of peace, can implore from Him upon humanity the great, indispensable gift of real peace. May the holy Mother of God answer us mercifully in this way, on this first day of the year, dedicated to her; may she accompany us in this way for the days which we are awaiting. Amen, amen.

—Homily on New Year's Day, 1976 (OR)

Mary's Role in the Plan of Salvation

Some days ago the 27th Italian National Liturgical Week, promoted by the Liturgical Action Center, ended in Bologna. The subject of the week was devotion to the Blessed Virgin today. The theme was examined in its doctrinal and liturgical expressions, as well as in the forms of popular and private devotion.

This is an event which deserves our attention because of the importance that piety towards Mary has both in relation to faith, since our Lady is at the center of the divine plan for our salvation, and in our everyday religious practice, since she, our Lady, makes the human mystery of Christ accessible to us.

The religion of our Lady is so close to us, citizens of the earth, that it easily makes devout even many of those who have no habitual familiarity in the mysterious field of prayer.

Who, if at all a Christian, refuses to whisper a "Hail Mary" in an hour of serious danger or intense grief, or to crown, as it were, a happy event of life? And at the same time the religion of the Blessed Virgin is by its nature so excellent that it opens the "gate of heaven" even to difficult spirits not always ready to cross its threshold. And all you faithful who, happily, make devotion to Mary one of the strong points of your spirituality, have you not realized that one can never know everything, or say everything about this humble handmaid of the Lord, this prophetic and royal woman, "humble and lofty more than a creature"? "De Maria numquam satis!" One can never say enough about her, even when adhering strictly to doctrinal truth and the poetry of the Gospel.

We say this, echoing the recent liturgical meeting so that, amid the religious apathy of our times, devotion to the Blessed Virgin may always be held in honor for our ecclesial world, both that inspired by Holy Scripture, theology and the recognized tradition of worship and art, and also popular, private and personal devotion (cf. *Lumen Gentium*, 27; *Marialis Cultus*, 24, etc.). We will find so many good and beautiful things in this Marian devotion: the commitment to a demanding and clear purity of morals, which are, unfortunately, in decay today; something to count on when faced with so many tribulations of ours, both individual and social, and above all a strong call to love and follow Christ, our only Savior, and always, therefore, a source of joy and confidence.

—*Angelus message, September 5, 1976 (OR)*

Joy, Sorrow and Glory in the Rosary

Many are the motives of our usual Sunday prayer and one enables us to make of it a garland. It is the rosary, this prayer so dear to Marian devotion, which has a special place in this month. The rosary is a popular form of prayer which we address filially to the Virgin Mary, as "Janua Caeli," the gate of heaven. We address to her, almost in familiar conversation, our repeated invocation, and thus let ourselves be introduced into the contemplation of the "mysteries." These are the scenes of the history of our salvation, dwelt upon in the light of her presence. It is she who lets us review the great scenes of the life of Jesus, as if they were superimposed on the humble events of our existence. It is a kind of spiritual television.

As you know, there are first the joyful mysteries. And here is one for us. In that green but so sorrowful island that is called Ireland, a hope is beginning to dawn: it is that of the prayer of the women of the North, Catholics and Protestants, that peace may flourish once more in that tormented people. The hope of justice and peace is reviving; and we thank the Mother of Christ for the Christian and civil joy that she is certainly obtaining for that blessed land and for those who share its suffering and its hope.

For the sorrowful mysteries: one wounds also ourself and the Church. It is the sentence inflicted on the Catholic Bishop of Umtali in Rhodesia, Most Rev. Donal Lamont, because of his intrepid defense of the human rights of equality and brotherhood in a country still subject to discrimination against the black population, the majority, by the whites. A sorrowful mystery, which we trust, invoking the Mother of Christ crucified, will be solved in terms of peace and honor.

And lastly there is a glorious mystery: we have been able to declare a "saint," that is, to canonize, a Spanish-Portuguese religious, who lived five centuries ago. She was the Foundress of a cloistered family, spread throughout the world, named after the Immaculate Conception, the most pure Virgin, blessed among all women, as we all know well. This noble lady, who lived for so many years with her beautiful face veiled, lets us contemplate, today, her face radiant with holiness and glory, and restores to us the idea of spiritual beauty, that of grace transfiguring the poor human face, today so often profaned by the false glitter of license and immorality. Let us admire, let us exult, and let us try to ensure that the halo of this new St. Beatrice, for that is her name, will pour forth also over our society rays of heavenly beauty, that of the Blessed Virgin.

—Angelus message, October 3, 1976 (OR)

Honoring the Mother of God

On these Sundays after Easter we will recite not the "Angelus," but the "Regina Caeli," as the liturgy of this period requires; consistent in discovering the glory and joy of the risen Christ reflected on the blessed person of the Virgin Mary.

We intend in this way to honor once more the very elect Mother of Jesus for the light that irradiates from her by virtue of the mystery of the resurrection of the Lord: the "lumen Christi" of the paschal night seems to have found the lamp from which it shines forth over the world and in the Church.

We likewise intend to atone with our humble and filial cry of honor for the blasphemous insults that are, unfortunately, sometimes hurled against our Lady, as we wish to exalt the dignity and purity of this immaculate Queen of heaven.

And we entrust to her our joy in being Christians, committed to faithfulness and love for the firstborn, the Redeemer of mankind, Jesus, her Son and our divine Brother.

—"Regina Caeli" message, April 17, 1977 (OR)

Pope's Prayer
to Mary Immaculate

Mary most holy,

Immaculate in your conception, beloved above all creatures, daughter of God the Father almighty, raised to the highest place in His merciful plan for all mankind.

You are the humble and admirable Mother of our Lord Jesus Christ, and therefore the Mother of God, that is, of the Incarnate Word, the Son of God and the Son of Man, our Savior. You are the most pure spouse of ineffable Love, the Holy Spirit, the mysterious Author of the Incarnation, which took place in your virginal womb.

Accept, O Mary, this act of our lively and unanimous devotion, whereby we wish to recognize and celebrate the choice that God has made of you, to be singularly blessed among all women, giving you a lofty and providential place in the plan of man's redemption. Virgin most pure, who cause to shine forth the transcendent ideal of human innocence and beauty, raising you up to be the perfect mirror of free obedience to the divine will, the incomparable yet accessible exemplar of faith, of hope, of love, a model for us of silent and joyous contemplation of the divine plan, and at the same time of solicitous and loving participation in the sorrows of human life.

Listen, O Mary, to our filial voice, echoing the sentiments of the whole Church on this tenth anniversary of the Second Vatican Council, and at the happy conclusion of this Holy Year, and we earnestly implore your special heavenly assistance in this critical hour for the spiritual and civil destiny of the world.

To you, spiritual Mother of the Mystical Body of Christ, which is the Church, we entrust the deliberate Christian commitment which we assumed with holy Baptism, and we confirm it in the spirit of renewal, which has marked the sacred Jubilee that we have just celebrated, and which must mark our witness as living members of the Catholic Church in the years to come.

To you, the Mother of the Church, we therefore entrust our commitment to reconciliation, which has likewise been strengthened during the Holy Year: reconciliation with God, reconciliation with all men our brethren, the longed-for complete reconciliation with all those who believe in our one Teacher and Redeemer, your Son Jesus Christ, ever increasing reconciliation through justice, liberty, cooperation among the different social groups, and finally reconciliation between the peoples and nations in a watchful and sincere spirit of security, collaboration and peace.

To you, O Mary, the fountain of life, we entrust the expectations of the young, who are restless in their search for a world more just and human, and we trustfully implore: guide their steps towards Christ, the firstborn of renewed humanity, so that in His light they may plan their endeavors and fulfill their hopes.

Queen of Mercy, O Mary, hear the laments of the suffering, the cries of the oppressed, the petitions of all who hunger and thirst for justice, and obtain for them relief from pain, recognition of their rights, and fulfillment of the desire for true freedom.

Holy guardian of the eternal Word, O Mary, hasten the hour of complete unity among all who confess Christ as the one Savior and Mediator. Handmaid of the Lord and daughter of Sion, look down upon your people, sprung from the faith of Abraham; Ark of the New Covenant, intercede for all those who have been redeemed by Christ but who as yet do not know the light of the Gospel.

Mother of the risen Lord and Mother of the reborn, O Mary, grant to us your children the spirit of the beatitudes, the love that believes all, hopes for all, the wisdom of the cross, so that, when death has been conquered, there may come the radiant dawn in which Christian expectation will be transformed into everlasting possession.

—December 18, 1977 (OR)

Daughters of St. Paul

IN MASSACHUSETTS
    50 St. Paul's Ave. Jamaica Plain, Boston, Ma. 02130
    172 Tremont Street, Boston, Ma. 02111
IN NEW YORK
    78 Fort Place, Staten Island, N.Y. 10301
    59 East 43rd Street, New York, N.Y. 10017
    625 East 187th Street, Bronx, N.Y. 10458
    525 Main Street, Buffalo, N.Y. 14203
IN NEW JERSEY
    Hudson Mall — Route 440 and
       Communipaw Avenue, Jersey City, N.J. 07304
IN CONNECTICUT
    202 Fairfield Avenue, Bridgeport, Ct. 06604
IN OHIO
    2105 Ontario St. (at Prospect Ave.), Cleveland,
       Oh. 44115
    25 E. Eighth Street, Cincinnati, Oh. 45202
IN PENNSYLVANIA
    1719 Chestnut Street, Philadelphia, Pa. 19103
IN FLORIDA
    2700 Biscayne Blvd., Miami, Fl. 33137
IN LOUISIANA
    4403 Veterans Memorial Blvd., Metairie, La. 70002
    1800 South Acadian Thruway, P.O. Box 2028,
       Baton Rouge, La. 70801
IN MISSOURI
    1001 Pine Street (at North 10th), St. Louis, Mo. 63101
IN ILLINOIS
    172 North Michigan Avenue, Chicago, Ill. 60601
IN TEXAS
    114 Main Plaza, San Antonio, Tx. 78205
IN CALIFORNIA
    1570 Fifth Avenue, San Diego, Ca. 92101
    46 Geary Street, San Francisco, Ca. 94108
IN HAWAII
    1143 Bishop Street, Honolulu, Hi. 96813
IN ALASKA
    750 West 5th Avenue, Anchorage, Ak. 99501
IN CANADA
    3022 Dufferin Street, Toronto 395, Ontario, Canada
IN ENGLAND
    57, Kensington Church Street, London W. 8, England
IN AUSTRALIA
    58 Abbotsford Rd., Homebush, N.S.W., Sydney 2140,
       Australia